Resilient Aging

Making the Most of Your Older Years

MIKE M. MILSTEIN

iUniverse, Inc.
New York   Bloomington

Resilient Aging
Making the Most of Your Older Years

Copyright © 2010 Mike M. Milstein

All rights reserved. No part of this book may be used or reproduced by any means, graphic, electronic, or mechanical, including photocopying, recording, taping or by any information storage retrieval system without the written permission of the publisher except in the case of brief quotations embodied in critical articles and reviews.

iUniverse books may be ordered through booksellers or by contacting:

iUniverse
1663 Liberty Drive
Bloomington, IN 47403
www.iuniverse.com
1-800-Authors (1-800-288-4677)

Because of the dynamic nature of the Internet, any Web addresses or links contained in this book may have changed since publication and may no longer be valid. The views expressed in this work are solely those of the author and do not necessarily reflect the views of the publisher, and the publisher hereby disclaims any responsibility for them.

ISBN: 978-1-4401-7588-6 (pbk)
ISBN: 978-1-4401-7590-9 (cloth)
ISBN: 978-1-4401-7589-3 (ebk)

Library of Congress Control Number: 2009937689

Printed in the United States of America

iUniverse rev. date: 11/10/2009

*To Annie Henry,
my resilient partner*

Resilient Aging:
Making the Most of Your Older Years

Contents

Chapter One   Living with Resilience in Our Third Age 1

My Retirement Story 2
Exercise: Retirement 8
Interest about Aging Is Growing 8
The Baby Boomers 10
Resilient Aging 11
- *Internal and Environmental Resiliency Building Factors*   13
- *Adversities and Responses*   15

Resiliency Elements 16
- *Positive Connections*   16
- *Clear, Consistent, and Appropriate Boundaries*   16
- *Life-Guiding Skills*   17
- *Nurture and Support*   17
- *Purposes and Expectations*   18
- *Meaningful Participation*   18

Who Should Read This Book 19
How This Book Is Organized 20

Chapter Two   Changing Perspectives about Aging 23

Aging Myths 24
- *Aging Can't Be Altered*   24
- *Aging Well Means Looking and Acting Young as Long as Possible*   27
- *Loneliness, Unhappiness, and Abandonment Are the Lot of Most Aging People*   29
- *Aging People Are Sexless*   30
- *Older People Are Past Their Most Productive Years*   31

Exercise: Aging Myths and You.. 36

How Aging Myths Have Developed 36

The Shift to Positive Images of Aging 40

Figure One: Alternative Pathways through Our Older Years 41

Our Older Years 41

Let's Move On... 42

In Closing 43

Chapter Three   Positive Connections 45

A Look at Positive Connections... 46

Exercise: Who Are You Connected With?... 49

The Importance of Connectivity for Aging People..................................... 50

Connectivity Is a Two-Way Street 52

Promoting Connectivity... 53
- Factors Related to Our Life Stage   53
- Factors within Ourselves   55
- Environmental Factors   57

Exercise: You and Connectivity 62

In Closing 62

Chapter Four   Clear, Consistent, and Appropriate Boundaries...... 65

Why We Need Clear, Consistent and Appropriate Boundaries to Guide Us in Our Older Years 66

Why Is It So Difficult to Develop Clear Boundaries for Aging? 68
- Society's Images   69
- Loss of the Known   70
- Medical Advances   71
- Coming to Terms with Our Mortality   72

Dealing with Boundaries: It's All about Your Perspective 73

- The Half-Empty Glass Perspective 73
- The Half-Full Glass Perspective 74

Exercise: What You See Is What You Get 76

Promoting Clear, Consistent, and Appropriate Boundaries 76
- What We Can Do 77
- Support by Others 80

Exercise: You and Clear, Consistent and Boundaries 83

In Closing 84

Chapter Five   Life-Guiding Skills 87

The Importance of Life-Guiding Skills 88

Exercise: Breathing Your Way to Calmness 91

Strategies to Develop Life-Guiding Skills 92
- Positive Attitudes 92
- Managing Transitions 93
- Gender Issues 94
- Responding to Change 94
- Seeking Life's Meaning 95

Pursuing Growth and Development 97
- Volunteering, Engaging in Leisure Activities, and Pursuing Hobbies   98
- Taking Care of Ourselves 98
- Managing Stress 100
- Reaching Out for Support and Intergenerational Connections 102
- Accepting Realistic Limitations 104

Exercise: You and Life-Guiding Skills 105

In Closing 105

Chapter Six   Nurturance and Support 109

The Importance of Nurturance and Support 110

Exercise: Do You Matter to Others? 113
- The Costs of Isolation 114

The Challenge of Establishing Nurturing and Supporting Relationships 115

Strategies That Promote Nurturance and Support 117
- *Develop a Positive Self-Image*   117
- *Risk Intimacy*   118

Encourage Positive Regard and Feedback 119
- *Foster Interdependent Relationships*   120
- *Replace Lost Relationships*   122
- *Develop Non-People Alternatives*   122
- *Select Caregivers Carefully*   123
- *Promote Positive and Caring Environments*   124
- *Use Political Power*   126

Exercise: Nurturance, Support, and You 127

In Closing 127

Chapter Seven   Purposes and Expectations 129

The Importance and Benefits of Purposes and Expectations 131

Exercise: How Do You Want to Spend Your Older Years? 136

Percent of Time Allocation by Categories 136
- *What Gets in Our Way?*   137
- *Environmental Barriers*   137
- *Internal Barriers*   139

The Good News: Older People Are Rejecting Society's Myths and Creating Meaningful Lives 142

Strategies for Developing Purposes and Expectations 143
- *Our Health*   143
- *Our Attitudes*   145
- *Our Ability to Plan and Act*   147

Exercise: Your Purposes and Expectations 150

In Closing 151

Chapter Eight   Meaningful Participation 153

Meaningful Participation: Why Is It So Important? 154

Exercise: What Meaningful Participation Means to You 157

Barriers to Meaningful Participation 157
- Negative Beliefs — 158
- Our Perceptions and Our Behaviors — 160

Strategies That Promote Meaningful Participation 162
- Positive Attitudes — 162
- Social Networks — 163
- A Balance between Reaching Out and Turning Inward to Reflect — 164
- Giving — 165
- Developing Supportive Environments — 168

Exercise: You and Meaningful Participation 170

In Closing 170

Chapter Nine   Putting It All Together 173

How I Have Applied Resiliency Elements 174

Resilient Living in Your Older Years 179

Planning for Resiliency 181
- Get Over Your Resistance to Change — 181
- Get Real about the Starting Place — 183
- Develop Your Vision — 184

Exercise: Clarifying Your Vision 185

Actualize Your Vision 185
- Create Meaningful Goals — 185
- Identify Strategies to Achieve Your Goals — 186
- Monitor and Assess Your Progress — 187

Keep the Vision Alive 188
- Enlist Support — 188
- Celebrate — 189
- Repeat the Cycle — 190
- Keep Learning and Changing — 190

In Closing 191

References 193

Chapter One

Living with Resilience in Our Third Age

Change your thoughts and you change your world.
—Norman Vincent Peale

Our lives can be roughly divided into thirds. During the first third, we grow up and become adults. During the second third, we pursue careers and raise families. Now, as longevity increases, particularly over the past century, many of us can realistically expect to experience as much as another third of our lives *after retirement*.

As we move through our middle years and pass on to our third age, we have a lot to think about. For example, we may worry about how we can care for aging parents and still arrive at our own older years without being exhausted and broke if we have to assist them financially and emotionally; we may hope for longevity but fear growing old; and we may dream of retirement but wonder what we will do with the ever-growing number of years we still have the potential to live.

How much do you know about aging? Do you have the information you need to prepare for the realities of your own aging years? Do you think you can age with energy, enthusiasm, and wellness? Or, on the contrary, do you think that aging is a time of the big "Ds"—decline, disease, destitution, and death? Do you even give much thought to your own aging, or is the prospect of aging so negative that you avoid thinking about it?

In recent years, we have learned a lot about the aging process. We have also learned a lot about the diverse ways

> *There is no "best" age in life. There's only putting the best life into your age.*
> —Gene Perret.

that people actually respond to the challenges of growing older. This knowledge can help us prepare for our own aging years if we make the effort to become acquainted with it. The more we know, the more we can make decisions and take actions that promote wellness rather than decline.

Our older years are likely to be challenging in many ways, including the possibility of financial stress, shifts, and changes regarding work and family roles, health problems, and the loss of longtime friends and family members through death. But as we synthesize our life's experiences and become wiser, it can also be a time marked by joy, caring, a deepening awareness of our humanness, and a chance to contribute to others in unique and meaningful ways.

This book is dedicated to helping you create a healthy and meaningful older life. It is based on the premise that we can do much to take charge of our older years if we are willing to learn and have the motivation, curiosity, and attitudes that support our potential for growth and development. It is also about helping you understand the challenges and opportunities that you are likely to experience in the last third of life, and how you can create and implement effective ways of responding to them.

> *Age is just a number and life is what you make of it.*
> —In The Middle" study, AARP, publication page

So, let's get started. To ground the discussion about the challenges of crossing the bridge into the third age, we begin with a brief look at the author's experience of transitioning into retirement. Then we will explore why there is currently so much focus on aging. Finally, we will introduce resiliency and the key resiliency elements that you can tap to improve your aging experience.

MY RETIREMENT STORY

Long before we reach our own retirement years, most of us develop images of what we think they might be like. In large part, these images are based on the experiences of others who have come before us.

> *Our conception of old age is a bad habit to which most of us have been conditioned too early.*
> —Ashley Montagu

My own first attitudes were formed based on observing how my father and grandfather chose to retire. Their choices and experiences provided both positive and negative images about retirement and aging.

My grandfather immigrated to the United States from Eastern Europe and struggled to make ends meet and support his family. He was not happy about having to work hard, so when the opportunity to retire came in his mid-sixties, he pulled out a rocking chair, sat on his front porch, and watched the world go by. He lived another twenty years but rapidly lost his energy and vitality, became forgetful, and coped with declining health. Formerly the family patriarch, it was not long before he became a bystander in the lives of his children and grandchildren.

> *The ultimate tragedy of life is not having lived fully when one is alive.*
> —Norman Cousins

What I saw was somebody I admired and cared about choosing to shut down his life. Even as a teenager, just starting out in the world of work, it seemed to me that his decision to lead a leisurely and sedentary life in his older years was probably not one that I would choose when my own time came to retire.

My father also worked hard, but he enjoyed the challenge. In fact, he continued to run his own business until he finally retired at the age of seventy-five. Once retired, he surprised everyone by initiating a variety of new activities, including travel, walking, fishing, and, as the oldest sibling, taking on the mantle of family patriarch. Always active in his synagogue, he extended these efforts after he retired, and he consciously reached out to support others, especially his children and grandchildren. He lived a full life,

> *It's true, some wines improve with age, but only if the grapes were good in the first place.*
> —Abigail Van Buren

relatively free of health problems, and died a happy man at the age of eighty-seven. Watching my father create an enthusiastic, energized, and expansive approach to retirement was impressive. Although I think he could have pursued his interests sooner if he had chosen to retire earlier, he still set a positive tone for me. Unlike my grandfather, who disengaged from life and rapidly declined physically and intellectually, my father grew and continued to develop in his older years.

These alternative images of retirement provided me with the insight that leading an active life *after* retirement would be more likely if I chose to lead an active life *before* I retired. Many years later, this is proving to be true. That is, the best predictor of how we will live after we retire appears to be how we lived before we retire.

> *To live a beautiful old age, you must live a beautiful youth, for we ourselves are posterity, and every man is his own ancestor. I am today what I am because I was yesterday what I was.*
> —Elbert Hubbard

My own work life was challenging and rewarding. After teaching a few years in a public school, I finished my graduate training and spent thirty-three years as a professor at two different universities. I was able to teach, pursue research and writing interests, take four interesting sabbaticals to different parts of the world, lead two academic departments, and interact with many extraordinary faculty members and students. At least in part because I switched universities about halfway through my career, my work life stayed new and vibrant right up to the time that I retired.

Still, there comes a time when we all begin to feel the urge to leave work behind and pursue other interests. I began to feel this tug in my late fifties. By the time I reached sixty, it was calling loudly, and I made a commitment to retire when I reached sixty-two, which was when I would be eligible to receive social security and a retirement annuity. It appeared that I

> *There is a time for departure even when there is no certain place to go.*
> —Tennessee Williams

would have sufficient resources to live a good quality of life without continuing to work for pay. I spent the next few years firming up my decision, sharing it with other faculty members, completing some unfinished research and writing projects, finishing graduate student advisement commitments, and thinking about the activities I wanted to pursue after retirement.

> *Good-bye tension. Hello pension.*
> —Retired teacher, anonymous

To my surprise, just getting through those last couple of years before

I retired and the first years after retirement were quite challenging. First, the closer the time came to retire, the more I found myself being marginalized by other faculty members in my department. I was always an active participant in department governance, but after announcing my retirement, I started to feel that my ability to affect decisions was slipping away. Those around me were moving on, and they started discounting me as a participant, knowing that they would be responsible for future events, and it would only be a short time before I was out the door. For the first time in my working life, I began to realize the meaning of the term "lame duck."

Second, shortly before I retired, I divorced and remarried. My new wife was also a professor and, at that time, actively engaged in her work. This led to some unexpected challenges. In the past, we'd shared similar work lives. After I retired, her life remained the same, but mine changed significantly. She continued to teach, write, and travel professionally for the next five years, until she also retired, while I experimented with how I wanted to spend my energies and time during retirement. Keeping our relationship positive and growing while traveling different paths required lots of discussion about expectations and behaviors. We made conscious efforts to find quality time to be together, which has provided a solid and positive foundation for our joint-retirement years.

Third, I found it extremely difficult to obtain the information that I needed regarding what retirement might be like. My university and the state's retirement board were helpful, once I figured out where to find the information, regarding nuts-and-bolts issues such as calculating monthly annuity payments, the cost of continuing health benefits, and how to close out my university activities. But they did not provide guidance about psychological issues—such as how to let go of my long-term academic role or how to shift my focus toward alternative activities that might be of interest in retirement. Nor were they of any help regarding emotional or spiritual questions that I might have or that I should have been encouraged to think about.

Fourth, after I retired, it was quickly made clear to me that I was no longer needed at the university. Initially, there was a flurry of activities, beginning with the ritual of cleaning out my office and ending with a wonderful farewell luncheon put on by my colleagues. I even got a gold watch from the university president. After these formalities were over, I fantasized that I would receive calls from my colleagues, asking for my advice and possibly my participation in current and emerging initiatives and challenges. I even rehearsed my responses. I would thank the callers but remind them that I was now retired and politely decline their requests. *But the phone didn't ring!* My former workmates had moved on, and I had to come to terms with the reality that I was not indispensable. I later discovered that many other retirees have experienced the same disillusionment.

Fifth, since I retired, I find that many people respond to me differently. Professors are granted lots of status. Their idiosyncrasies are usually viewed positively by students and others in the academic community. However, it has been my experience that once a professor retires, these same idiosyncrasies are viewed less positively. For example, now people often are impatient if they think I am responding too slowly. They even send signals that say they think I may be incapable of understanding what they are saying. I also get nonverbal messages that they are not

> *The young man is deliberately odd and prides himself on it; the old man is unintentionally so, and it mortifies him.*
>
> —Richter

terribly interested in the stories that seemed to be liked (or was it "tolerated"?) when I shared them with my graduate students. I have concluded that the higher we were in the pecking order of the working world, the more difficult it may be to make the necessary adjustments about how we are treated in our older years. In fact, blue-collar workers frequently adjust to retirement better than executives and professionals do because they experience much less difference in their lives before and after retirement than do those with higher work life status.

Sixth, I needed to sort out how I was going to spend time once I left the world of work. I have now been retired for a decade and have accumulated many new life experiences. I have experimented with and discarded some activities, including learning how to play the piano and taking extended camping trips, neither of which have been as satisfying as I thought they would be. However, other activities have turned out to be more engaging. For example, I have spent quality time cultivating my interest in photography, gardening, and cooking. I have also continued practicing those things I really enjoyed doing professionally, such as consulting and writing, while dropping things that are not so attractive, like having to stay in town to teach semester-long courses.

Finally, I have also discovered that life is neither harder nor easier in retirement. It's just different. It is becoming clear that I will continue to face positive and negative challenges as long as I live. On the positive side, I entered into a wonderful marriage; I continue to have engaging and satisfying relationships with friends; I have become an enthusiastic student of, and presenter about, the aging process; and I have more control about how I spend my days.

On the negative side, I was devastated by the loss of my adult son a few months after I retired. Soon after that, age-related challenges to my body, whose sturdiness I had always taken for granted, began to creep up. For example, I was diagnosed with prostate cancer, a health challenge that affects many men at my life stage, and my loved ones and I have had to cope with this new reality. So far, I have been doing well, but I am aware that there will likely be further health-related challenges as I grow older.

As I moved through the transition from work life into retirement, I have come to look forward to my life in the third age with curiosity and enthusiasm. I now have a notion of what it is all about. It's about having the same sense of mission and purpose that I had throughout my career. It's about continuing to be part of a community of caring people. It's about remaining healthy. It's about living fully until I die. And it's about facing my own mortality.

These concerns are not unique to me. Each of us has to come to terms with growing older. In fact, the point of describing my story is to emphasize that getting ready for retirement and living a quality life during our older years is challenging. My experience has led me to conclude that, as the saying goes, old age may not be for sissies, but with forethought, vision, and planning, it can be highly satisfying, productive, and a time of growth and development.

> *Retirement is just another word for finally getting your priorities straight.*
> —Anonymous

> ## Exercise: Retirement
>
> You probably are reading this book because you either expect to retire soon or you have already moved into retirement. No doubt my story is different from yours. This activity is intended to help you reflect on your own story.
> 1. What issues came up for you as you prepared for retirement?
>   A.
>   B.
>   C.
> 2. Who are the role models (positive or negative) who have been important in shaping your thinking about retirement? What images about retirement did they leave you with?
>
>   *Role Models*   *Images*
>
>   A.
>   B.
>   C.
> 3. If you have already retired, what positive and negative challenges have you had to deal with?
>
>   *Positive Challenges*   *Negative Challenges*

INTEREST ABOUT AGING IS GROWING

Growing old was the exception rather than the rule until the past century. At the birth of America in 1776, average life expectancy was thirty-five. A hundred years later, this increased to forty. By 1900, it jumped to forty-seven. The trend toward greater longevity has been even more dramatic since that time—increasing to seventy-four for men and seventy-nine for women by the end of the twentieth century. The news is even better for those who have already reached sixty-five because the odds are that they will have even more years of life. For men who have reached sixty-five, the average life expectancy is almost eighty-three. For women who have reached sixty-five, the average life expectancy is now more than eighty-four.

To put these longevity increases into perspective, think about two facts: First, the average years added to our lives over the past century, "represent two-thirds of all gains in life expectancy achieved since the emergence of the human species!" (Coles, 1996, p. 236) Second, according to former UN Secretary-General Kofi Annan, for the first time in history, people over sixty will soon outnumber people under sixty worldwide. These dramatic changes have occurred in a small fraction of the time the human species has existed.

We have also seen a major shift in the age profile of the overall population as the average life span has increased. Over the past years, we have gone from a youthful society, with the largest age group composed of people from birth through their twenties, to an older society, with many more individuals in their forties through their eighties. The sixty-five-plus group has increased most rapidly: In 1900, about 4 percent of the U.S. population was sixty-five or older. Today this group has more than tripled! Further, demographic forecasts indicate that this age group will continue to expand faster than all younger age groups and will likely reach about 20 percent, or one in five, of all Americans during the twenty-first century. Most telling, the fastest growing age group in our society is made up of those who are ninety or older (Rowe and Kahn, 1999).

> *This increase in the life span and in the number of our senor citizens presents this nation with increased opportunities: the opportunity to draw upon their skill and sagacity—and the opportunity to provide the respect and the recognition they have earned.*
> —John F. Kennedy

Other developed countries are experiencing comparable shifts toward older populations. In fact, Canada, the Scandinavian countries, the United Kingdom, West Germany, Switzerland, Austria, Belgium, Italy, Greece, Luxembourg, France, Finland, Hungary, the Netherlands, and Spain have a larger percent of citizens in the sixty-five-plus group than does the United States. In large part, the demographic shift in these developed countries is the result of a dramatic decline in infant mortality over the past century due to medical breakthroughs, particularly the development of vaccines for such scourges as smallpox. It also is related to improved living conditions, particularly to healthier sanitation practices, as well as improved medical support throughout the lifespan, which reduces, or at least postpones, disease-related deaths among aging populations.

THE BABY BOOMERS

The baby boomer generation is enormous and, as a group, holds significantly different beliefs and expectations about their aging years than those of generations that preceded them down this road. The baby boomers, an influential group comprised of those who were born between the end of World War II and 1964, constitutes the largest single birth cohort in U.S. history. During the nineteen years before 1945, which were most notably marked by the Depression and war, there were 49 million births. During the nineteen years that formed the baby boomer generation, there were 76 million births. Equally dramatic population shifts have occurred to one degree or another in other countries.

By the time the baby boomers reached adulthood, developed countries had shifted from agrarian small-town and small-business societies to urbanized, large-city, highly technical postmodern societies . There was also an increasing intergenerational physical separation as nuclear and multigenerational families gave way to separate households for aging parents and families spread widely, dispersing across the landscape.

The boomers matured while lifestyle choices expanded and became more available to those interested in exploring alternatives to the values and priorities of preceding generations. For example, in the United States, a period of relative economic stability provided boomers with the resources to experiment. It was also a period of political instability, marked by civil rights confrontations, the turmoil of the war in Vietnam, political assassinations, and unprecedented stresses on traditional sources of societal values—the home, the church, and the local community. The result is that many members of this large generation now approaching retirement have lived alternative lifestyles, traveled extensively, and are accustomed to speaking out and reshaping society.

The first wave of baby boomers is now turning sixty-five, the traditional age of retirement. This is a stark reality in itself, but based upon responses given when asked, many baby boomers do not plan to wait until they reach sixty-five to retire. The impact of this large group of people arriving at the portals of retirement in the near future is likely to be significant. Whether boomers will actually be able to retire before or even at sixty-five is not certain. It will be difficult for them to do so if their resources are depleted. The boomers are often referred to as the "sandwich generation" because many of them have to lend support to two generations. They are sandwiched between their parents, who are living much longer than any prior generation of older people, and their children, who are not always financially able or enthusiastic about leaving home during these complicated and expensive times. Current recessionary realities will compound the difficulty of retiring early.

> *And in today already walks tomorrow.*
> —Samuel Taylor Coleridge

However, whether they retire early or postpone retirement, the baby boomer generation is becoming an aging population. It has always been a major adjustment for individuals to move from the world of work to living in retirement, but for the baby boomers, it is likely to be even more challenging because, as a group, they have lived more diverse and more materialistic lives than any preceding generation. If past behavior is indicative of future behavior, the baby boomer generation will likely follow Dylan Thomas's admonition: "Do not go gently into the night." As Ram Dass says (2000, p.87), they "have been raised in a consciousness-seeking era and will refuse to be viewed as irrelevant." In short, the boomers are surely going to challenge current beliefs and expectations about how we age and how we connect with family, friends, and community.

RESILIENT AGING

The purpose of the book is to help you respond effectively to the challenges that come your way as you age. That's what resiliency is all about: responding to life's challenges in ways that make you stronger and healthier. Being resilient means having the skills and behaviors that are supportive of your ability to grow and develop.

It also means being able to exhibit positive attitudes about aging. In fact, there is a strong linkage between our perceptions about aging and our longevity. According to one study, people who have a strong will and are positive about their aging years live, on average, seven and a half years longer than people with negative self-perceptions (Levy et al., 2002.). Positive attitudes and strong wills are characteristic of resilient people. They see possibilities where others see limitations.

> *I dwell in possibility.*
> —Emily Dickenson

> *Things are not as bad as they seem. They are worse.*
> —Bill Press

> *The greater part of our happiness depends on our dispositions and not our circumstances.*
> —Martha Washington

Resiliency, which was initially developed as a concept to help children cope better, is relevant for people at all life stages. Let's begin by laying out the basic philosophy of the resiliency approach. For starters, when you look at a glass that contains liquid filling 50 percent of its volume, how do you see it? Is the glass half-full or half-empty? Which image do you resonate with? If you see the glass as half-empty, you probably tend to be pessimistic, concentrating on what is missing and what *can't* be. If you see the glass as half-full, you probably tend to be optimistic, concentrating on what exists and what *can* be. How we perceive things shapes our lives powerfully.

> *The hopeful man sees success where others see failure, sunshine where others see shadows and storm.*
> —O S. Marden

As you think about growing older, how do you see your life? Is it "half-empty," full of problems to be solved, hazards to be avoided, and issues to be surmounted? Or is it "half-full," with challenges that excite you, get your adrenaline going, and motivate you to grow? How much we enjoy our lives and respond to challenges is highly dependent on our perceptions. If we interpret challenges

> *We cannot change the inevitable. The only thing we can do is play on the one string we have, and that is our attitude.*
> —Charles Swindall

negatively, we live in fear and try to avoid them as long as possible. If we interpret challenges positively, we live with enthusiasm and feel capable of responding to them effectively.

People who view challenges positively are *resilient*. They may encounter as many or even more hardships in their lives as those who view things negatively, but they cope with them differently. They bounce back from adversities, learn from experiences, solve problems effectively, develop new skills, and gain self-confidence in the process. The ability to bounce back is characteristic of resilient people at all life stages, from youngsters to centenarians.

Internal and Environmental Resiliency Building Factors

Each of us, whether young, middle-aged, or older, has the potential to respond to life's dynamics with resilience. Yet there are great variations in how people actually do respond. Some of us collapse when faced with adversity. Some barely survive. Others, the resilient ones, use their experiences to grow stronger.

These different responses can be traced to two important set of factors. The first set of factors has to do with *the personality and characteristics of the individual.* Some of the important individual factors include the following:

- being of service—giving to others or to a cause
- having good decision-making and problem-solving skills
- being sociable and having the ability to form positive relationships
- having a sense of humor
- having a positive view about the future
- being spiritual or believing in a greater power
- having self-confidence

The extent to which we possess these characteristics is based partly on genetics and our personalities, but it is also partly based on life experiences and how we respond to them. Some of us may exhibit most of these characteristics, while others may exhibit few, if any, of them. However, our situations and our capabilities are not set in stone. There is much that can be done, such as learning skills, dropping dysfunctional habits, and learning new and more effective ways of coping, to shift the balance toward greater resiliency.

The second sets of factors has to do with our *surroundings* or *environments*. These include our families, neighborhoods, the organizations we participate in, and the communities in which we live. These surroundings can either support our growth and development or deplete it, in which case it may be necessary to find ways of avoiding, changing, or leaving them. We are

> *What is the use of a house if you haven't got a tolerable planet to put it on?*
> —Henry David Thoreau

energized when we live in environments that are supportive of our growth and development needs as resilient individuals. Characteristics of supportive environments include the following:

- promoting interactions that are high in warmth and low in criticism
- encouraging supportive relationships
- promoting shared responsibilities and mutual support
- encouraging achievement and success
- encouraging the development of positive values
- providing opportunities for decision making and meaningful involvement

If we live in depleting environments, they will probably hinder our ability to behave resiliently. But even in such environments, it may be possible to see potential, or at least to overcome constraints. As Viktor Frankl, who survived the unspeakable conditions of the concentration camps in World War II, notes (1959, p.162), "Life is potentially meaningful under any conditions." For most of us, though, it would probably be extremely difficult to remain optimistic and motivated if we had to live in such a negative environment. In contrast, if we are able to shape environments that are responsive to our developmental needs and that support our efforts, we are more likely to fulfill our potential to live resiliently.

Adversities and Responses

Adversities that are likely to come our way as we grow older include:

- changes that come with retirement or loss of a job
- the deaths of our parents
- losing our spouse or other long-term partner
- losing friends
- health problems
- declining resources

Depending on the extent to which we have honed our resiliency capabilities, our responses to these adversities can vary along a continuum from loss and submission to growth and success.

> *Old age transforms or fossilizes.*
> —Marie von Ebner-Eschenbach

To clarify how these responses might play out let's look at how we could respond to the loss of friends who have moved away or died. A *dysfunctional response* would be to continue to grieve for an extended time and avoid relating to others because of the pain that might be associated with further losses. A *survival response* would be to hold even tighter to our remaining friendship group, even though it will inevitably shrink and disappear with time. A *comfort zone response* would be to make efforts to replace such losses with new friends who appear to be like those who we have lost. A *resilient response* would be to connect with new and different kinds of people, including individuals who are older and younger than we are, with the hope that in allowing a broader scope of interests and insights into our lives, they will become more meaningful. It might also include developing an interest in new activities that involve learning and creativity, which might also lead to the development of new friendships.

Resiliency, in short, is about the ability to confront life's challenges in ways that lead to improved capabilities and a more positive sense of self. To live resiliently, we need to have a clear understanding of its underlying elements, be honest about our current state of development regarding them, and find ways of closing the gap between our current realities and our preferences. Let's begin by defining the key elements.

Resiliency Elements

Resiliency is an important foundation for living a meaningful life. It applies to all of us, whether young, middle-aged, or older (Blum, 1998; Higgins, 1994; Werner and Smith, 1992). Resiliency can be especially important in our third age, when physical abilities decline and we are challenged in ways that require us to be proactive and adaptable. If we learn to apply the following six resiliency elements (Milstein and Henry, 2008) and live in supportive environments, we will probably experience positive, healthy, and meaningful lives.

> *Life is like riding a bicycle. You don't fall off until you stop pedaling.*
> —Claude Pepper

Positive Connections

With the possible exception of hermits and monastics, we all need positive, healthy, and supportive connections with others and the core values that underlie them if our lives are going to have meaning and value. We need to connect regularly with people, activities, programs, organizations, and communities. These connections help us clarify and decide about such critically important issues as who we are, what is important to us, and how we want to live. We need to maintain and nurture positive connections established earlier in life and seek out new ones that help us achieve a sense of belonging and meaning as we change and age.

> *He who has a why to live can bear almost any how.*
> —Friederich Nietzche

Clear, Consistent, and Appropriate Boundaries

Our expectations and the expectations of others greatly affect our behaviors. These expectations, or boundaries, may be communicated formally and in writing, as in the case of laws, policies, and procedures. They may also be communicated informally, verbally or nonverbally, as in the case of behavioral preferences that are transmitted through cultural norms. Either way if they are clear, consistently enforced, and appropriate to our needs and abilities, they can serve as a safety net, providing a sense of security as well as guidance for appropriate behaviors. However, as we move out of our midlife years and into our aging years, many of the boundaries that had formerly shaped our behaviors may no longer be relevant or appropriate. For example, as we grow older we leave behind highly structured and established expectations about how we should relate to family and work. We need to create new and appropriate boundaries that provide the security to continue our growth and development in later life. Because society does not provide clear behavioral expectations for older people, many of the boundaries regarding how we live and relate have to be self-developed.

> *To enjoy freedom we have to control ourselves.*
> —Virginia Woolf

Life-Guiding Skills

It requires more than good intentions to navigate life's twists and turns. It takes skill and competence in such areas as goal setting, planning, problem solving, decision making, communicating, and conflict management and resolution. It also requires being able to cultivate reflective practices and spirituality. We need to develop these skills, hone them through experience, and apply them flexibly as life progresses and conditions change. Developing these life-guiding skills as we age is especially important because we live in a society that does not frequently honor the needs of elders or recognize their abilities.

> *The supreme end of education is expert discernment in all things—the power to tell the good from the bad, the genuine from the counterfeit.*
> —Samuel Johnson

Nurture and Support

We are most fully alive when we are in caring relationships. Our sense of self-worth and value is enhanced when we give and receive unconditional positive regard, encouragement, and trust. We thrive in relationships with relatives, friends,

> *The deepest principle of human nature is the craving to be appreciated.*
> —William James

and those charged with our care when they are reciprocal, nurturing, and supporting. Everyone, from newborn babies to centenarians, needs to be loved and cared for, to be touched and held. Babies draw love and care like magnets, but aging people typically don't get such lavish attention. Learning how to ask for and receive nurturance and support is important. Likewise, being able and willing to give support to others is quite important for our sense of well-being.

Purposes and Expectations

Meaning is life's driving engine. Clarity of purposes and the expectations and motivation that can help us achieve them provide the impetus to respond to life's challenges. Without meaningful purposes and expectations, we are likely to become alienated, which can leave us adrift, with little ambition beyond survival. Our parents and others established

> *Lord grant that I may always desire more than I can accomplish.*
> —Michelangelo

many of our purposes and expectations earlier in life. These include expectations that we will become independent and financially secure, find a mate, raise a family, and do well in our chosen lines of work. As middle age gives way to older age, many of these purposes and expectations no longer serve as motivators. Instead, we have to go inward, reflect, and identify new expectations that are relevant to us and can serve as a foundation for positive living in our older years.

Meaningful Participation

We need to feel connected to our families, friends, organizations, and the communities we live in. Meaningful participation reminds us that we are social beings and not alone, that we have something to offer for the greater good, and that we have the responsibility to give something back in return for all the nurturing we have received. Older people have the time, life experiences, and knowledge to participate meaningfully. However, although there is much need for their energies and talents, they may not

> *Few things help an individual more than to place responsibility on him, and to let him know that you trust him.*
> —Booker T. Washington

know how to make the appropriate connections required to do so or be invited to participate. Many are left with too much time and energy and no productive outlets. We need to make it more feasible for people at this life stage to participate and contribute to others.

These are the basic elements, or building blocks, that constitute resiliency. They are highly interrelated, so as we are becoming more effective in applying one, we are also likely to improve our abilities to apply others. For example, when we develop stronger connections, we also serve our need for nurturance and support. Similarly, when we clarify our boundaries, we gain a sense of security and the confidence to take the risks required to develop meaningful purposes and expectations.

WHO SHOULD READ THIS BOOK

RESILIENT AGING: Making the most of your older years is written for everyone considering or already in retirement. This includes anyone who goes through the transition from paid work or household management responsibilities into retirement. Those anticipating retirement are most likely people in their mid-fifties or beyond. If you are in this group, the book can help you pay attention to and reflect about the life stage that you will soon be

> *Forty is the old age of youth; fifty is the youth of old age.*
> —French proverb

entering, anticipate the kinds of challenges and opportunities you will encounter, and plan how you will respond to them. If you have already retired and are presently dealing with aging challenges, it can help you think through specific issues that you may want to respond to more effectively. Whether you are part of the preretirement group or the postretirement group, the contents of the book can help you become more resilient and improve the odds that you will lead a meaningful life in your older years.

While most of the information that is presented in the book has been developed in the United States, the challenges that are explored and the strategies we can use to respond to them are applicable elsewhere. Many other countries are experiencing the same kind of growth of their older populations, and they are concerned about how they will be able to support them, provide them with necessary medical services, and find creative ways of tapping into the wisdom and energy represented by this life stage group.

This book is not about dealing with the most extreme problems associated with aging. For example, it doesn't deal in any detail with disease and rapid decline. There are books that focus on topics such as Alzheimer disease, dementia, care-giving, and end-of-life issues. Such topics are important, especially if you or loved ones are confronted with them. However, they are beyond the scope and intent of this book.

How This Book Is Organized

Chapter 1 has introduced the purposes of the book, described the author's movement into retirement, and laid out the resiliency framework that will be used throughout the book. Chapter 2 explores obstacles to becoming more resilient. It portrays basic demographics and trends concerning aging, how aging has been viewed over time, the myths that hinder our potential to age well, and changes over the past few decades that are causing us to alter our thinking about aging. It focuses on clarifying and adding to the shift in thinking about aging, away from negativity and toward positiveness and potentiality.

Chapters 3 through 8 explore, in some depth, the six resiliency elements introduced in chapter 1: Positive Connections (chapter 3); Clear, Consistent, and Appropriate Boundaries (chapter 4); Life-Guiding Skills (chapter 5): Nurturance and Support (chapter 6); Purposes and Expectations (chapter 7); and Meaningful Participation (chapter 8). Each chapter includes a brief story about an aging person who needs to develop skills to meet a resiliency challenge, information about the meaning of the specific resiliency element, obstacles to being able to exhibit it during our older years, and strategies that can be employed to get past these obstacles to lead a good-quality and meaningful life. The six resiliency elements are presented in separate chapters so readers can focus on them one at a time. However, in reality, the six elements are complementary and overlap each other. When we practice strategies that improve our behaviors regarding one resiliency element, we will probably also find that we are growing more capable regarding other resiliency elements. For this reason, there will also be some purposeful redundancies in the strategies suggested.

Finally, chapter 9 begins with a return to the author's continuing aging journey—the resiliency challenges I am dealing with and the plans I am pursuing—but mainly it focuses on suggestions for planning and decision making that can help you build your own resiliency foundations.

Most chapters include brief exercises. You are encouraged to complete them because they can promote reflection, help internalize the information presented, and increase insights about your own aging situation. The intent of the exercises, in other words, is to help you discover meaning that is unique to yourself and leave you in a better position to apply the strategies that are presented in the book.

Finally, it should be noted that it is not necessary to read the book in the order it is presented. You may want to explore some particular resiliency elements more than others. Each chapter stands on its own and can be read separately, so feel free to choose those that are of most interest to you.

Chapter Two

Changing Perspectives about Aging

*Youth, large, lusty, loving—youth, full of grace, force, fascination.
Do you know that Old Age may come after you
with equal grace, force, fascination?*

—Walt Whitman

Many people have mixed feelings of anticipation and dread as they grow older and move into their third age. Negative realities include the possibility that aging will be a time of loss, health problems, decline, loneliness, and withdrawal from society. Even the word retirement conjures up negative images. Webster defines "retire" as a time "to go away... to go to bed ... to give up ..." On the

> *It is a mistake to regard age as a downhill grade toward dissolution. The reverse is true. As one grows older, one climbs with surprising strides.*
>
> —George Sand

other hand, there is the potential to age positively; it can be a time of growth and development, freedom from past responsibilities, opportunities to build a legacy, synthesize life's meaning, and become a wise elder. Viewed this way, we might think of "protirement" rather than retirement.(Hudson, 1991, p. 175), which is about throwing "yourself ahead into a new blend of work and other activities. Protirement is a positive plan for a new chapter in life, emphasizing possible options and personal renewal."

How we think about our aging years is often influenced by our societal beliefs and, more specifically, what those around us believe. We need to know about these beliefs and place them in proper perspective or they may hinder our ability to live with resilience. Chapter 2 presents persistent negative myths about aging that have become part of our belief system and summarizes the mounting evidence that is shifting our thinking toward more positive perceptions about growing older.

AGING MYTHS

Society's myths about aging can inhibit growth and development during our older years, but only if we choose to believe them. As Morrie Schwartz, a wise old man who was dying from Lou Gehrig's disease, reminds us "You have to be strong enough to say if the culture doesn't work, don't buy it." He also says, "Create your own… The big thing—how we think, what we value—those you must choose yourself." (Albom, 1997, pp. 37 and 155),

> *Few people are capable of expressing with equanimity opinions which differ from the prejudice of their social environments.*
> —Albert Einstein

> *Of all the self-fulfilling prophecies in our culture, the assumption that aging means decline and poor health is probably the deadliest.*
> —Marilyn Ferguson

The first step in making such choices is to become aware of the myths, learn the facts, and develop a realistic perspective about the aging process. Frequently stated myths and the facts that contradict them include the following:

Aging Can't Be Altered

When Bismarck ruled over Germany in the latter part of the nineteenth century, pressure was building for the creation of a safety net for older people. He decreed seventy to be the age for retirement. Why seventy? Apparently because very few people lived beyond that age! He later changed the age of retirement to sixty-five, which soon became the age that many countries chose as the first year of eligibility for newly initiated government-supported retirement programs. At the time of passage of the Social Security program in the United States in the 1930s, average longevity was less than sixty-

> *Old age is not so bad when you consider the alternative.*
> —Maurice Chevalier

> *Growing old is no more than a bad habit which a busy man has no time to form.*
> –Andre Maurois

two, and most of those who lived beyond this average still worked because they had no pensions. Today the average longevity is much older, and only a minority of people who are over sixty-five are still fully employed in the work force.

With government-sponsored retirement programs in place, it was not long before sixty-five came to be viewed as the beginning of the last stage of life, the time when disease and despair set in. In fact, "disengagement theory," a model of aging that was popular until a few decades ago, holds that we are meant to withdraw, or disengage, from involvement with others in the community and society as we age. This process, which is supposed to enable society and older individuals to prepare for the inevitable process of incapacitating disease, decline, and, ultimately, death, dominated the beliefs and behaviors of gerontologists until the late twentieth century (Cumming and Henry, 1991).

This negative stereotype has persisted despite the fact that life expectancy has increased and is continuing to do so at an unprecedented rate. Men, on average, can now expect to live into their late seventies, and women, on average, can expect to live into their early eighties. These added years might be marked by decline, disease, and depression for some, but not for most of us. For example:

> *Each age from first to last is good in itself and may be lived, not only well, but happily.*
> —Edmund Sanford

- Private and public pension funds have expanded older citizens' choices well beyond those of prior generations of aging people.
- Access is now widely available to travel, enjoy entertainment, and pursue adult learning opportunities.
- Medical advances are slowing the onslaught of chronic diseases and leading to treatment programs that mitigate their worst effects if they do develop.
- Local and national programs have been created to support the needs of aging individuals.
- Innovative housing patterns, which keep older people connected and involved, have been developed.
- Better diet and exercise programs are keeping the aging population more fit.

In short, it is now more feasible for aging people to remain healthy and enthused about their lives. Given such changes and the growing "use it or lose it" attitude of older people, the stereotype that aging can't be altered is in retreat. For example, the belief that senility is an inevitable accompaniment of aging is being seriously questioned. Senility, especially in the severe form of dementia known as Alzheimer's disease, though devastating when it does occur, is limited in the number of elderly people it affects. In fact, only about 5 percent of people who are in their sixties and about 20 percent of those over eighty suffer from Alzheimer's disease. Further, better early diagnosis and treatment breakthroughs are likely to have a positive impact on the incidence and severity of Alzheimer's disease.

> *My father told me "You gotta keep progressing or you decay." So rather than atrophy mentally and physically, I just kept forging ahead.*
> —Clint Eastwood

Gerontologists are also providing evidence that while older people may lose a little speed in their ability to respond, there is scant evidence of significant memory loss or, for that matter, of declining intelligence as we age. In fact, a recent study of centenarians in New England indicates that decline, dementia, and disease are not inevitable (Perls and Silver, 1999). As a group, centenarians in that study demonstrated amazing mental and physical capabilities, adaptability, optimism, and a sense of purposefulness about life. They moved through their sixties, seventies, eighties, and nineties with the same high level of health and enthusiasm.

> *As long as you are curious, you defeat age*
> –Burt Lancaster

Finally, there are positive changes going on regarding our thinking about the lifecycle. In just one generation, "new passages" are leading to the potential to live actively for a longer time into our older years, perhaps even lengthening our midlives by as much as a decade (Sheehy 1995). Reflecting these changes, new language is being created: The *young-old*, the majority of whom are in their

> *There is more felicity on the far side of baldness than young men can possibly imagine.*
> —L. P. Smith

sixties and seventies, are those who are healthy and active. The *old-old*, most of whom are in their eighties and beyond, are people who are physically limited and in decline. Of course, this is not a rigid division. There are people in the sixties and seventies who have declined and moved into the old-old group, and there are people in the eighties and beyond who have managed to retain the vibrancy and health of the young-old.

Our negative perceptions of aging may be due to memories of our mothers and fathers growing older, many of whom aged faster under more limiting conditions than we are experiencing. As a result of positive changes, including medical breakthroughs, improved dietary habits, physical exercise options, social connectivity, and greater financial security over the past few decades, our experience will probably be different from theirs.

Aging Well Means Looking and Acting Young as Long as Possible

Society perpetuates the myth that aging is about loss of vitality, attractiveness, and the ability to make meaningful contributions. The implicit message is that old age is nothing more than the absence of youth. This myth is supported by an aggressive media that glorifies youth and encourages us to do everything possible to hold on to any vestige of our younger days for as long as possible. For example:

> *The secret to staying young is to live honestly, eat slowly, and lie about your age.*
> —Lucille Ball

- Facial creams are supposed to be applied and plastic surgery is supposed to be pursued when our inevitable skin wrinkles appear.
- Gray hair, especially among women, is supposed to be hidden behind hair dye.
- Vigorous participation in sports activities, even in direct competition with younger people, is supposed to be pursued, despite the reality of aching joints, brittle bones, and declining muscular structures.

The constant bombardment of youth vs. aging dichotomies provides persuasive evidence that society perpetuates the mythology that aging is all about the loss of youth. For example, a content analysis of television shows and magazine articles concluded that mass media rarely portrays images of people older than sixty-five, except when focusing on problems and the various miracle drugs and cosmetics that can be used to avoid aging, or at least slow it down, as long as possible. Images of older people engaged in active lives are conspicuous by their absence (Friedan, 1993).

> *Youth is a disease from which we all recover.*
> —Dorothy Foldheim

These same media outlets reserve an inordinate amount of space and coverage that features young adulthood as desirable and the prime time of life. The Clairol slogan "You're not getting older, you're getting better," sends the message that using Clairol to color our hair will make us look younger, which is what is implied by "getting better." The success of Clairol's approach taps into our urgency to find the fountain of youth and avoid aging at all costs. Popular films such as *On Golden Pond, Cocoon, Peggy Sue Got Married, Back to the Future,* and *Golden Years* also support the myth that quality aging is about experiencing a second childhood.

> *Every man desires to live long, but no one would be old.*
> —Jonathan Swift

When George Burns said, "We have to get older, but we don't have to get old!" he didn't mean that we have to turn the clock back. He meant we have to move into our older years with the purpose, enthusiasm, and creativity equivalent to that which we experienced at earlier stages of our lives, but which are more appropriate for the life stage we are living now. The sixty-five-plus group has unique opportunities for challenge, learning, and development that are *only* available to those with understanding, life experience, maturity, and time, all of which are usually in short supply among the young.

> *We push the clock back and try to prolong the morning, over-reaching and over-straining ourselves in the unnatural effort ... In our breathless attempts we often miss the flowering that waits for the afternoon.*
> —Anne Morrow Lindburgh

Every life stage is unique and must be measured on its own terms: Childhood, adolescence, young adulthood, middle age, and older life all have their own challenges and possibilities. It is far better to focus on active engagement with the life stage demands and possibilities that one is currently experiencing than to fixate on earlier life stages that are no longer part of our reality.

> *I don't want to get to the end of my life and find that I lived just the length of it. I want to have lived the width of it as well.*
> —Diane Ackerman

Loneliness, Unhappiness, and Abandonment Are the Lot of Most Aging People

At best, this image of aging conjures up visions of elders with too much time and too little to do. At worst, it conveys a picture of frailty, institutionalization, and wasting away until the grim reaper arrives to collect his due. No wonder so many people avoid thinking about aging, which is costly because it keeps us from planning for and living the meaningful life that can be experienced in our aging years.

> *We who are old know that age is more than disability. It is an intense and varied experience, almost beyond our capacity at times; but something to be carried high.*
> –Florida Scott-Maxwell

Fortunately, the reality for most older people is quite different from the mythology. For example:

- At any given time, only about 5 percent of people over the age of sixty-five live in institutionalized settings such as nursing homes, and only about 10 percent of people over the age of sixty-five will ever live in such settings.
- Those who experience institutionalization typically do so near the end of life.
- The average age of admission to nursing homes is eighty years old.
- Only about 5 percent of older people are constantly bedridden.
- Older people get fewer acute illnesses than younger people do.

- Approximately 70 percent of older people live with at least one other person.
- Eighty-six percent of older people typically see one or more of their relatives on a weekly basis.
- Older people tend to watch less TV on a regular basis than do people in their twenties.
- Although there is widespread belief that adult children of older parents do not care to spend time with them, the reality is that intergenerational contacts are more frequent than we may think. Even when large geographic distances exist between generations, modern technologies such as the telephone, the Internet, and computer-driven audio and visual systems have proven to be effective vehicles for maintaining important connections.

There are also ever-widening opportunities for older citizens who might otherwise succumb to the myth of loneliness and despair to socialize. These opportunities include government-sponsored initiatives such as senior centers; outreach programs like Meals on Wheels; and privately driven initiatives such as senior housing cooperatives, other types of residences, and social clubs. There are also many volunteer programs, ranging from mentoring youngsters to providing support for community development. In addition, for those of us who have extended, multigenerational families, there are many opportunities to provide a variety of support roles.

Aging People Are Sexless

> *It's so long since I've had sex, I've forgotten who ties up whom.*
>
> —Joan Rivers

This stereotype holds that most aging people have little interest or ability to engage in, active sex lives. It is perpetrated through endless jokes and negative imagery. Older men are often portrayed as "over the hill," impotent, and unable to perform sexually, while older women are depicted as sexually undesirable, having lost their libido, and being uninterested in participating in sexual activities. Just as damaging are the negative attitudes held about older adults who *are* sexually active, which ranges from surprise and shock to disbelief and disgust about such "unseemly" behavior of "dirty old men" and "shameless old women."

Given such attitudes, one might conclude that older people should not pursue active sex lives or, at the very least, be as discreet and private as possible about doing so. Such thinking can be devastating to one's self-image and beliefs about the ability to perform. It may even contribute to depression.

Just as in younger groups, sexual interest and opportunities for sexual activities vary among older people. There are also unique problems of aging that impact one's sexuality, such as illness, institutionalization, widowhood and the earlier mortality of males. A particular issue for men has been concern about the ability to achieve an erection. But now, with aids like Viagra readily available, many older men are overcoming what was thought to be an irredeemable dysfunction.

Even with challenges such as those noted above, there is little evidence to support the belief that older people are sexless. In fact, the few studies that have been done on the sexual attitudes and behaviors of older people provide evidence that stereotypes of older people, regarding sexual attitudes, interest, and activity, are inaccurate. For instance:

- Ninety percent of older people are positive about unmarried and widowed people engaging in sexual activities.
- Ninety-seven percent report liking sex.
- Eighty percent believe that sex is good for their health.
- Seventy-five percent think that sex is as good or better than it was when they were younger.
- Four out of five men who are sixty or over are physically capable of sex.
- About 15 percent of men and women exhibit an increasing level of sexual activity as they age (Friedan, 1993; Cox, 1993).

Many aging men and women are interested in and actively engaged in sexual activities. Further, older adults who choose to remain sexually active often find themselves more able than many younger people to relax, be patient, and engage in physical

> *Rather than believing that you'll be less likely to have sexual relationships as you age, envision yourself as sexually deserving now and in future years. You can still have sex and enjoy it.*
>
> —Amye Dean

intimacy that is shared and comfortable to both partners. The payoff, in short, is more than worth the effort to maintain and cultivate an active sex life during our older years.

Older People Are Past Their Most Productive Years

A commonly held view is that physical stamina and energy are depleted and creative juices dry up as we age. Our contributions to family, community, and society are deemed to have run their course. Those who try to stay actively engaged are often told to slow down, enjoy the leisure of their "golden" years, and leave responsibilities for the world in the capable hands of younger people. Unless they remain in the work force, even when older people do manage to stay involved, their contributions are often discounted because they are not paid activities.

> *A person is not old until regrets take the place of hopes and plans.*
> —Scott Nearing

The reality is that few older people choose to retire to the rocking chair and the TV set. In fact, many remain as active and productive as they were earlier in life. Some even find that this life stage provides opportunities to be more creative and contribute to society in ways that were not available to them during earlier life stages. With parenting responsibilities completed, many of us in our sixties and beyond have the time and resources needed to explore and nurture our interests. For example, we might cultivate our gardens, pursue hobbies like photography or painting, or volunteer our services in our communities. Still others might wish to work part-time or full time, or maybe even start new careers. Those who elect to remain at work are usually viewed as highly valued employees because, in comparison to younger workers, they have established re-

> *Life is a romantic business. It is painting a picture, not doing a sum—but you have to make the romance, and it will come to the question how much fire you have in your belly*
> —Oliver Wendell Holmes

> *Years may wrinkle the skin, but to give up interest wrinkles the soul.*
> —Douglas MacArthur

cords of low absenteeism, high retention rates, and on-the-job experience. We might also pursue adult learning opportunities, including participating in individually guided activities, adult education courses, and Elderhostel-type experiences, or even enrolling in undergraduate or graduate degree programs.

With experience, enthusiasm, and creativity, we have the potential to make our older years a time of exceptional creativity. According to Cohen (2001, p.12), creativity is "the flame that heats the human spirit and kindles our desire for inner growth and self-expression." In fact, creativity may be as important as physical stamina and a good diet. It encourages a positive outlook and a feeling of well-being, which, in turn, supports the effective functioning of our immune system and our continued good health.

> *"Old age" should be a harvest time when the riches of life are reaped and enjoyed, while it continues to be a special period for self-development and expansion.*
> —Ashley Montagu

The point is that older people do not have to think of themselves as being past their most productive years. Many individuals have left an indelible mark on society during their aging years:

> *Life is either a daring adventure or nothing. To keep our faces toward change and behave like free spirits in the presence of fate is strength undefeatable.*
> —Helen Keller

- Konrad Adenauer was chancellor of Germany at eighty-eight.
- Clara Barton founded the American Red Cross and was still its president at the age of eighty-three.
- George Burns was working as a comedian and was booked for a performance at the London Palladium when he died at one hundred.
- Coco Chanel headed a fashion design firm at eighty-five.
- Agatha Christie was still writing books when she died at the age of eighty-six.
- Winston Churchill served his last term as England's Prime Minister at the age of seventy-seven.

- Will Durant won the Pulitzer Prize for history at age eighty-three.
- Mahatma Gandhi didn't even turn to the political arena until he was fifty, and he went on to lead his people to nationhood until he was murdered at age seventy-eight.
- Sir John Gielgud's acting career extended from the 1920s through the 1990s.
- Martha Graham, a modern dance pioneer, danced until she was seventy-five and continued to do choreography until she was ninety-six.
- Alfred Hitchcock was still making cutting-edge films when he was in his eighties.
- Oliver Wendell Holmes was a Supreme Court judge when he was ninety.
- Henri Matisse, the gifted painter, continued to improve on his craft despite suffering life-threatening disabilities, right up to his death at the age of eighty-five.
- Michelangelo was still creating masterpieces when he died at the age of eighty-nine.
- James Michener, who produced an amazing quantity of fiction, was still working when he died in his early nineties.
- Golda Meir continued to be a leader of her party after stepping down as prime minister of Israel at the age of seventy-six.
- Grandma Moses began painting at seventy-nine and was still painting at one hundred.
- Pablo Picasso was still creating innovative artworks when he died at ninety-one.
- Jeannette Rankin, who was the first female in Congress, led five thousand women to Washington, D.C., to protest the war in Vietnam when she was eighty-seven.
- George Bernard Shaw was still writing his unique body of work at the age of ninety-four.
- Helena Rubinstein ran a beauty empire and wrote her memoirs in her nineties.
- Albert Schweitzer was still working with lepers in Africa at the age of ninety.

- Mother Teresa served the poor and infirm of Calcutta for many years, right up to when she died at the age of eighty-seven.
- Mao Tse-tung was still leading China, the most populous country in the world, in his eighties.
- Mae West spent more than six decades on the stage and in films and was still professionally active in her eighties.
- Frank Lloyd Wright's most creative works began in his sixties and did not end until he finished designing the Guggenheim Museum at the age of ninety, a year before his death.

> *Nothing great was ever achieved without enthusiasm.*
> —Ralph Waldo Emerson

These well-known individuals continued to be creative in their older years. Some of them didn't even find their creative stride until late in life, and many pursued their passions until the day they died. Besides being extraordinary individuals who enriched the world, they served as positive role models for others.

Creativity is not reserved for the famous. There are countless "ordinary people" around the world, who live vigorous, productive, and creative lives. They may not get the notice of the famous, but they operate on the same basic belief that life is to be lived to its fullest. You probably know older people in your own family, neighborhood, and community who make the quality of life for others richer while they pursue their own passions. Each of us has special gifts and talents that are ours alone. All that is required is for us to choose to develop and apply them.

> *I'm afraid I'm an incorrigible life-lover and life-wonderer and adventurer.*
> —Edith Wharton

Exercise: Aging Myths and You

Often we are not consciously aware of the impact aging myths have on us. Before we can move past them, we need to bring them from the unconscious to the conscious level. For each of the five myths we've explored, can you identify any examples of statements or images you recall from the media, casual encounters in stores or on the street, or from friends and family members that support these myths?

Myth	*Examples of Statements or Images*
Aging can't be altered.	
Aging well means looking and acting young as long as possible.	
Loneliness, unhappiness, and abandonment are the lot of most aging people.	
Aging people are sexless.	
Older people are past their most productive years.	

How Aging Myths Have Developed

It may surprise you to know that these myths were not part of the dominant belief system until late in the eighteenth century. Why did they come about, and are they immutable? If we are going to change our thinking about aging in more realistic and healthier ways, we need to learn how these myths took root.

Positive attitudes about aging predominated until the nineteenth century. During that time, there were few older people. For example in the United States the *average* age was sixteen,

> *That which seems the height of absurdity in one generation often becomes the height of wisdom in another.*
> —Adlai Stevenson

and only 2 percent of the population lived to be sixty-five or beyond. Older people were revered, at least in part because it was an accomplishment just to reach this life stage. But the respect given to older people was not only a matter of longevity. It was also because aging individuals who possessed land, which was the major source of wealth, kept control of this resource almost until life's end. Retirement was rare among those who persisted. More typically, they simply worked until they died. Because they stayed engaged, it follows that the important and powerful roles in society were reserved for elders. They had extensive life experiences, and it was a time of nation building. The wisdom of elders was sought to keep things moving. Not surprisingly, even fashion encouraged the young to emulate the old—to the point of donning gray wigs.

> *Old men and comets have been reverenced for the same reason: their long beards and pretense to foretell events.*
> —Swift

Attitudes about aging became increasingly negative in the late eighteenth century and remained that way until near the end of the twentieth century. Following the American and French Revolutions, the authority attributed to older individuals started whittling away. Fashions changed, and the young no longer tried to dress or look like their elders. As the population that was sixty-five and over increased from 2 percent in the 1770s to 10 percent in the 1970s, being older became less special. Derisive language about old people—e.g., old gaffer, old fogey, and old guard—was coined. The declining veneration of the old was accompanied by an increasing emphasis on the importance of the young to the growth and future of society.

> *Probably at no period and in no culture have the old become completely rejected as in our own country, during the last generation.*
> —Lewis Mumford

The Industrial Revolution also played a part in the shifting of attitudes. Leaving farms and small towns, people streamed into newly created factories. It was not long before aging workers were deemed obsolete and were reminded that they might not be up to their assigned tasks. Strict retirement ages were put into effect, and many workers were fired before they even reached these arbitrary retirement ages.

The twentieth century saw the rise of complex organizations, mass production, an expanding role of government in the lives of its citizens, and, as noted, a rapid shift of the population away from rural settings and into cities. Planning and regulation soon took hold, and aging became viewed as a "social problem."

Old-age pension plans were introduced because many older people were poor at the outset of the twentieth century. In fact, many private and regional pension plans were created before national governments established funded support systems for their older citizens. Whether private or public, pension plans contributed significantly to the reduction of poverty among the elderly.

Until recent decades, lifecycle researchers ignored the aging years. The pioneers of lifecycle study initially paid little attention to the older age group. For example, Erik Erikson (1986) identified and labeled this life stage "Integrity vs. Despair," or "Wisdom," but he paid relatively little attention to it until he reached his own aging years. Daniel Levinson (1978) identified "Late Adulthood" as the fourth season of one's life, but he only provided detailed information about life in the first three "seasons"—childhood, early adulthood, and middle adulthood). Gail Sheehy (1995) also neglected this later lifecycle stage until 1995, when she wrote *New Passages*.

The medical world began to take note of the unique concerns of the aging population early in the twentieth century. The creation of the field of geriatrics in 1912 led to a focus on disease and decline among the aging, creating a negative portrait of aging. However, much of the information that was initially gathered came from people who were residents of nursing homes. This skewed conclusions about the problems and potentials of older people.

> *An old error is always more popular than a new truth.*
> —German proverb

By the mid-twentieth century, the field of social gerontology was established, bringing important sociological and psychological perspectives to the study of the aging process. Gerontologists soon differentiated between normal and pathological aging. As the field grew and became more differentiated, it began to focus on dispelling the aging myths that have constrained our ability to conceive of aging positively. More recently, geriatric specialists have begun to look at the general population of older people and are focusing more on the vitality and wellness that many aging people continue to exhibit well into later life decades.

As a result of the preponderance of studies that focused on the negative aspects of aging, two theories that remained popular through most of the twentieth century promoted images of aging as decline followed by death. **Disengagement theory** holds that the task of older age is to face incapacitation and death, a rather fatalistic approach at best. **Activity theory** argues that "normal" aging calls for maintaining middle-aged activities as long as possible, which is another way of saying avoid growing older until it becomes impossible to do so. This is a no-win game: With each passing year, it becomes more and more difficult to cling to middle age behaviors. More important, it is questionable that this is even a good idea. Each life stage, including older age, has its rites of passages, difficulties, challenges, rewards, and potential for learning. Looking backward with yearning to past life stages depletes the energy and focus we need to move through life's transitions and into our new life stages.

> *Old age is like a plane flying through a storm. Once you're aboard there's nothing you can do about it.*
> —Golda Meir

> *The past should be a springboard, not a hammock.*
> —Anonymous

More objective theories began emerging during the 1970s. Two in particular were debated widely: **Continuity theory** emphasizes that as we age, we are likely to be guided by the skills and attitudes that were acquired in earlier life stages. In this regard, we discard activities that we didn't enjoy or excel at and tenaciously hang on to those we enjoyed and were good at. This may provide a foundation for planning, but it leaves scant room for adult learning, which is needed to develop new skills and promote creativity as we age. **Age stratification theory** focuses on the distinctive characteristics of a particular age group, and how it relates with other age groups in society. The problem is that this assumes that individuals in any particular age groups are more similar than dissimilar. The reality is that people become more differentiated rather than more similar as they age.

Mike M. Milstein

THE SHIFT TO POSITIVE IMAGES OF AGING

As more people live longer, the urgency to understand the potentials of our aging years becomes greater. For example, in the United States, having expanded from only 4 percent of the population in 1900 to almost 13 percent by 2000, the sixty-five-plus age group has become a force to be reckoned with. It is no accident that *Modern Maturity*, the monthly publication of the American Association of Retired Persons (AARP), which is dedicated to serving the interests of older people, has become the most widely distributed magazine in the country. Larger, more highly educated, and wealthier than former generations of older people, this group is making its presence known and pressing for a reassessment of the meaning of aging.

We're off to a good start, but we still have a way to go. We have created healthy alternatives to the negative models that dominated earlier. The focus has shifted from problems to potentials in our older years. We are changing our image of aging from a time of disease, loneliness, and insufficient financial resources, or as a time to relax and consume, to a time of opportunities to grow, develop, help others, and experience a deeper meaning of life.

> *People should think things out fresh and not just accept conventional terms and the conventional way of doing things.*
> —Buckminster Fuller

We still need to identify and respond to the problems associated with aging, but real as they may be, they represent only part of the aging picture. We need to maintain a realistic balance in our thinking about the problems *and* potentials of this life stage. For too long, we focused 80 percent of our attention on 20 percent of our reality, fixating on the downside of the aging process. While we all will die, there is a good chance that most of us will remain healthy and energized until near the end of our lives.

> *We know what we are, but we know not what we be.*
> —William Shakespeare

We might experience three different aging paths in our own older lives.

Figure One:
Alternative Pathways through Our Older Years

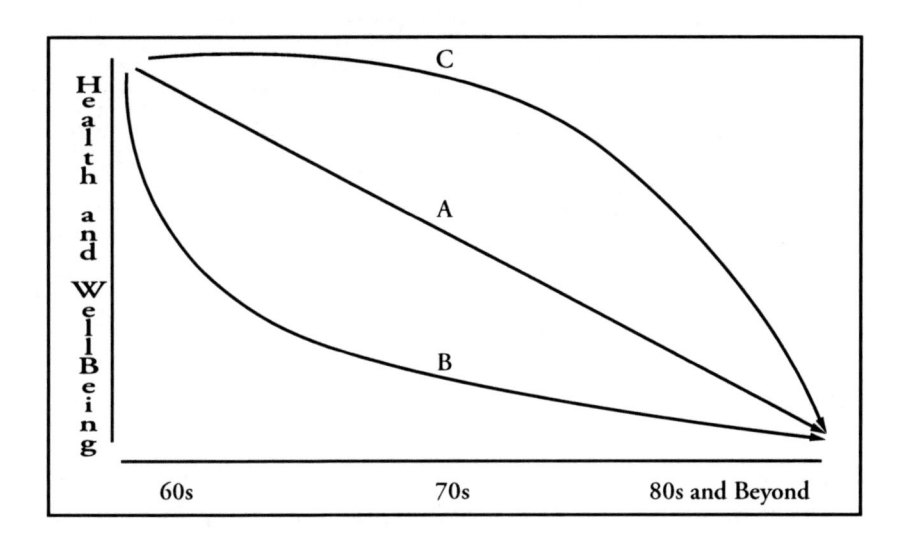

[Graph showing Health and Wellbeing on the y-axis and age ranges (60s, 70s, 80s and Beyond) on the x-axis, with three curves labeled A (steady decline), B (rapid decline), and C (gradual decline near the end).]

Our Older Years

As Figure II.1 indicates, we might decline along the A path at a steady downward pace over the length of our third age, if we let gravity take its course and do little to remain engaged with a meaningful life. Or we might decline rapidly along the B path because of mental and physical challenges such as Alzheimer's disease or severe osteoarthritis and hang on at a low functioning level for many years, making life quite difficult for ourselves and for our caretakers. Or we might be fortunate enough to travel the C path, relatively free of such diseases, making positive choices to stay physically and emotionally healthy so we can remain vitally engaged until shortly before we die. The myths of aging would have us believe that many of us will follow the A or B paths. However, the reality is that, in ever-growing numbers, most aging people are following the C path. There is much to cheer about as this reality becomes clearer.

> *It is amazing what ordinary people can do if they set out without preconceived notions.*
> —Charles F. Kettering

Mike M. Milstein

Let's Move On

We are beginning to understand the possibilities of aging. For example, we have learned much about prevention and remediation of disease and other health-related challenges in our older years. We are also doing a better job of helping older people combat loneliness and find ways of connecting with others. However, there is much more we can do to help elders grow more deeply and fully. In our fast-paced society, we tend to move quickly but not reflectively, with the result being a lack of understanding about the legitimate and important roles that elders can play in our society. If we age wisely and share our wisdom, we can gain a renewed sense of purpose, motivation, and inner peace (Shachter-Shalomi and Miller, 1995).

> *At first we want life to be romantic; later on, to be bearable. Finally to be understandable.*
> —Louise Bogan

> *When an old man dies, a library burns down.*
> —African proverb

Most so-called primitive societies intuitively understand the importance of their elders' contributions and reserve honored and sacred places for them in their communities. This has also been a widely accepted understanding for thousands of years in Eastern societies. Hindu tradition, Buddhist philosophies, and Taoist beliefs all place central importance on the role of elders. They hold that it is only in our older years that earthly struggles are calmed and the understanding and wisdom required to synthesize life's lessons flower within the individual and can be tapped for the well-being of one's community. Similarly, the Kabalah, which guided much of early Jewish thinking, holds that our ultimate goal should be to reach a stage wherein the self becomes one with the divine

> *Old age is winter to the unlearned. To the learned, it is harvest time.*
> —Yiddish proverb

> *There is only one solution if old age is not to be an absurd parody of our former life, and that is to go on pursuing ends that give our existence a meaning.*
> —Simone de Beauvoir

and provides light for the world. In Jungian archetypal terms, elders have the potential to become "magicians," who can live in harmony and help restore the world to wholeness and balance.

The point is that although there has not been much discussion about it in the West, there is indeed a rich history of forethought about the ripening world that is available to older people, and the ways that their growth and development can fulfill them and be important to their communities.

In Closing

As we age, our fondest hope is to be healthy, connected with others we care about, remain actively engaged in meaningful activities, and have the resources required for a decent quality of life. Most of us can experience the special qualities of aging that are available at this life stage. We can grow spiritually, synthesize our lives, develop deeper meaning about our existence, and come to grips with our mortality in ways that make living more meaningful and richer. Most of us have the capacity to age well, but to do so we need to develop positive attitudes and learn effective coping strategies. It takes effort to make the transition from our midlife experiences to the realities of aging, but the payoffs can be large.

> *Society is always taken by surprise at any new example of common sense.*
> —Ralph Waldo Emerson

How can we develop holistic strategies that improve our chances of aging effectively? How can we expand our thinking beyond our current level of understanding to encompass the deeper meanings associated with aging? There are no clear-cut answers to these important questions, but resiliency practices appear to be a good place to start. As we present these practices in the next six chapters, you will probably find that, to one degree or another, you already exhibit many of them. Most of us can profit by expanding upon the abilities we already possess and learning different approaches and strategies that can enhance our knowledge, skills, and abilities to age well.

Chapter Three

Positive Connections

We ought to think that we are one of the leaves of a tree, and the tree is all humanity.
We cannot live without the others, without the tree.

—Pablo Casals

Where has everyone gone? Sam, who was in his mid-sixties, had been wrestling with this question for several years. His network of caring people, a large group at one point in time, and one that he had come to take for granted, was thinning out rapidly. Most of his co-workers seemed to have moved on and had little time for him since he retired a few years ago. His parents were dead. His five brothers and sisters were scattered around the country, and some of them were dealing with serious health issues. On top of all this, he had been divorced for a decade, and friendships with other couples, much of it based on the dynamics of raising families, either held little interest for him or were less available to him. His children were striking out on their own and had moved away in pursuit of careers and family development. He also was coming to realize that community activities that were important to him during his earlier life stages, such as volunteering at his children's schools and serving on advisory committees at community centers, no longer interested him. Sam realized that the tried and true relationships of yesterday were slipping away. He felt alone and lonely, rudderless in the turbulent sea of life. All the givens were slipping away. He felt confused and frightened and began to question his value and place in the larger scheme of things. Where did he fit in? How would he satisfy his need for relationships?

Sam didn't give much thought to positive connections until they were drying up. After he was divorced, his parents died. Then he retired and lost his daily connections with people at work, many of whom he liked and cared about. Trying to fill the void, he turned to brothers, sisters, friends, and his own children, only to find that they had moved on and were preoccupied with their own lives. As long as he'd had a support system at work, he hadn't put much energy into maintaining family and friendship ties. Not surprisingly, without nurturing, many of these relationships had become superficial or were lost over the years.

Just as important, his involvement in the community had lapsed. Earlier in life, he believed that it was essential to set a good example for his children, so he participated in community affairs and became known as someone who cared. In return, he felt connected, valued, and a part of something meaningful. However, as time passed and his children grew up, he shifted his focus toward more personal interests. Now he was transitioning into his older years, and if they were going to be meaningful, he needed to rebuild positive connections in his life.

Without strong and meaningful connections, we are likely to feel removed from our past, confused about our present, and unclear about our future. This is especially true at the later stages of life, but this is also a time when we may have less energy and patience for building meaningful connections. Like Sam, we all need positive connections that can enrich our lives. The more we develop and maintain such connections, the more we will know who we are, where we've been, and where we are going.

Connectivity provides the foundation upon which the rest of the resiliency elements can be built. Creating meaningful boundaries, providing life-guiding skills, promoting nurturing and support, clarifying purposes and expectations, and expanding meaningful participation all require the development and continued maintenance of connective structures and processes.

How can we maximize the probability that we will have positive connections as we age? Chapter 3 focuses on this important issue. We'll begin by clarifying the meaning of "positive connections," and how aging is influenced by this important resiliency-building element. Then we will explore strategies that can be used by individuals, groups, organizations, and communities to establish, maintain, and promote positive connections.

A Look at Positive Connections

We all need solitude sometimes, but few of us want to be isolated from others all the time. We are connective beings, which is another way of saying we need to relate to others. We need to know that we are part of something bigger than ourselves, part of a larger order that helps us establish a sense of purpose and meaning for our lives. To connect effectively with our families, friends, and communities we need to know what is valued and what is not valued, what is appropriate and what is inappropriate.

People who show a will to live and are positive about aging, both of which are promoted by connectivity, can add years to their lives. In fact, as noted, one study concluded that such people will live, on average, seven and a half years longer than those who don't exhibit these characteristics (Levy et al., 2002). People who are disengaged are also more likely to encounter health problems, including life-threatening challenges such as heart attacks and cancer.

> *A light heart lives longer.*
> —William Shakespeare

Knowing the importance of connectivity is one thing. Making it happen is quite another thing, especially for aging people in our fast-paced, highly materialistic, youth-oriented society. This has been particularly true since the Industrial Revolution led to the creation of large, complex organizations, where older workers are often criticized and bypassed when their ability to produce is in doubt. As a result, many older people have found themselves discounted, isolated, and pressured to resign.

In earlier, more agrarian, times, elders could find a place for themselves by returning to family farms, or small towns, where they could put their energies to good use for their families and their communities. It is more difficult for many of us to be connected today than it used to be. Living on farms or in small communities, which promotes connectivity, is no longer available to most of us. Our intergenerational family connections have also become more tenuous as our adult children move long distances in search of career opportunities. In addition, we are uprooting ourselves as we age, heading for warmer climates and for the growing number of planned older-residents-only communities. For all these reasons, many of us are at risk of being on our own and isolated.

One thing is certain: If opportunities for *positive* connections are difficult to find, people will find *negative* connection opportunities because we need to be connected to maintain a sense of our place and believe that we matter to others. For example, we might connect with other elders who are dissatisfied and complain about their unhappy lives, or we might place demands on our adult children for their time and support.

Exercise: Who Are You Connected With?

This activity can help you reflect about your past and current connections—e.g., with family, friends, and other community members.

1. Take a few moments to think about positive connections that you have experienced in your life. List those that you view as being important to you. What is it about each of these connections that made them important?

Important Connections   *What Made Them Important*

A.

B.

C.

D.

E.

2. What are some things you've done that work well for you in your efforts to develop positive connections?

A.

B.

C.

D.

3. What do you need from connections now?

4. Are your connections meeting these needs?

5. If your connection needs aren't being fulfilled, what do you think you need to do?

Mike M. Milstein

The Importance of Connectivity for Aging People

The importance of involvement and positive connectivity with family, friends, and community for older people cannot be overstated. As we grow older, many of us come to realize that life is not just about material success and ego satisfaction. We find ourselves placing a higher priority on the importance of connectivity and on the quality of our lives. We need basic resources for survival and for a modicum of comfort to enjoy life, as well as self-esteem and self-confidence. But we also become

> *The trouble is, old age is not interesting until one gets there. It's a foreign country with an unknown language to the young and even to the middle-aged.*
> —Mary Sarton

more aware of the importance of connectivity and community and the satisfaction this provides, as well as the unique roles that we can play as elders with our families, friends, and community when we set aside the priorities of earlier life stages.

Former President Jimmy Carter (1998) refers to the blessings and responsibilities that elders have to connect and be of benefit to others. For example, we can help the homeless, mentor youngsters, or support other elders who are less able. When we follow President Carter's advice, we enhance our sense of relevance and purpose. But to do so, we have to move beyond purposes—such as being self-supporting adults, finding mates, raising children, and pursuing careers—that were appropriate for earlier life stages. These purposes lose their motivational intensity once we are past midlife.

The challenge is to recognize when to move on to new motivators that may be more appropriate for our aging years. As we shed the temporal responsibilities and priorities of youth, young adulthood, and middle age, we need to find new ways of connecting and become open to new possibilities,

> *Eighty percent of success is showing up.*
> —Woody Allen

responsibilities, and priorities. When we leave the expectations and requirements of earlier adulthood behind, we can focus on connecting in ways that allow us to synthesize life's experiences, mentor, explore spirituality, become wiser, and share our wisdom as culture bearers.

This is new territory for most of us. Besides making the commitment to do what is required, we also need support, which means connecting with others who are on the same pathways. We also need to maintain supportive relations with family, friends, and others.

For older people who are going through one of life's biggest and least understood transitions, connectivity is critically important for the promotion of a positive sense of self. It also helps us come to terms with our mortality and our place in the larger order of things. Connectivity can bring our attention to meaning and purpose in powerful ways, helping us clarify what is important and what makes our lives meaningful. As we age, the days we have left decrease, but realizing this can provide the impetus to make each remaining day more meaningful.

> *The goal of human life is constructing an architecture of the soul.*
> —Simone Weil

> *Our life ... the less there is left of it, the more precious it becomes.*
> —Goethe

Connectivity in our older years can lead to distinctly different benefits for men and women. Most men in our competitive, male-dominated society live constricted definitions of what it means to be a man—posing as heroes and keeping their need for intimacy at arm's length. However, once past midlife and moving into retirement, many of the restrictive expectations of society ease up, and it becomes more feasible for men to explore their full humanness, including exhibiting attributes that have traditionally been identified as "female" qualities. These attributes include nurturing, empathizing, and expressing feelings, all of which many men have been encouraged to suppress at earlier life stages. As men age, they have opportunities to let go of constricted definitions of what it means to be male. They can learn to express themselves more fully and connect more frequently with women as well as other men who have learned how to express these important attributes.

Women have also been assigned limiting roles earlier in life. They were expected to support others around them, particularly their husbands and families if they were married and had children. The feminist movement has made great strides to expose the inappropriateness of the limitations established by these roles, but many women still set aside their own dreams and hopes in favor of supporting those around them. With age and the completion of earlier life tasks, many of these expectations are lifted. The empty nest syndrome and the transition into later life can be a time of liberation and celebration, a time for women to explore their full selves, master a skill, take up a profession, and relate more completely with others.

> *And the face I have now, I've really earned.*
> —Susan Sarandon

CONNECTIVITY IS A TWO-WAY STREET

In many agrarian societies, elders maintain their traditional role as culture bearers, helping communities focus on core values. They model healthy ways of relating and provide guidance about positive and appropriate behaviors and norms.

Over the years, elders in urbanized and industrialized countries have been losing this important role. The loss of this elder role is directly related to the decline in intergenerational connectivity. The more society segregates its elders, the more it loses the important resources that only those at this life stage can provide. When this happens, there are significant costs, both to society and elders. In fact, it can be argued that the well-being of society is dependent upon returning older citizens to their centrally important place as culture bearers. The importance of this elder role is multifaceted. Given the opportunity and the support to play this role, elders can do the following:

> *The presence of elders is like the shade of a tree.*
> —Hindi proverb

- preserve the collective memory that helps following generations understand the significance of the past to the well-being of communities and society today and tomorrow
- mediate conflicts dispassionately, using their life-experiences to promote balance and harmony among families and communities

- share their experiences and knowledge in ways that can be of help to others
- keep extended families together by providing support for adult children and grandchildren
- model what healthy and meaningful aging looks like for younger people
- share values that have guided their lives and might be important for others to consider
- help younger people understand how we can relate to each other positively, the importance of expressing our gratitude and joy for the opportunity to be alive, and the reality and significance of our mortality

Promoting Connectivity

Connectivity doesn't just happen. People who are highly and positively connected work at it. They see themselves as capable and worthy and are empathetic about the needs of others. They value relationships but are not dependent on them for their sense of self. They are relatively adaptable and seek new connections, which they view as positive and interesting challenges to be experienced, rather than as threats to be avoided.

> *Old age is full of enjoyment if you know how to use it.*
> —Seneca

What contributes to the development of these personal attributes? While there is no one formula that fits all of us, some basic factors support and sustain our ability to connect. These factors, which need to be nurtured and refined, are discussed below: *our life stage, within ourselves*, and *in our environments*.

Factors Related to Our Life Stage

We need to come to terms with where we are in life if we hope to connect positively. Some of us are perpetually fascinated with youthful ways. Others fixate on motivations that are typical of our middle-aged years

> *The face you have up to age thirty-five is the one you are born with: After thirty-five, it's the face you have made.*
> —Attributed to Abraham Lincoln

and resist leaving them behind in favor of living fully and appropriately during our aging years. Yet others may accept the realities of aging, but do so with resignation and dread, constricting the likelihood of growth and development.

Those who accept aging as part of life and see opportunities that become available at this stage make connectivity a priority. They do so because they know the following:

Transitioning into their third age is tricky business, but for those who manage it well, the rewards can be extensive. To do so, we need to connect with older people who can serve as positive role models and with others from our own age group to journey with as peers. Life is a series of developmental phases. *Midlife Reevaluation* is shaped by a sense of crisis, the time when we have to establish meaning and satisfaction as our work lives begins to run out. *Liberation*, which typically occurs during our sixties and early seventies, can lead to a sense of personal freedom and an unleashing of our creative potential. *Summing-Up* has to do with focusing on the development of the deeper meaning of life and sharing our wisdom. *Encore*, the final stage, takes place as we focus on finding ways of affirming our passage through life and celebrating our achievements (Cohen, 2001). Moving through one developmental stage to another is not guaranteed, but it is more likely to occur if we are connected with others who are experiencing the same challenges, as well as with those who have already navigated these tricky waters and can help us in our efforts to do the same.

- Many of us become aware of the importance of mentoring and sharing our wisdom at this life stage. This recognition, in turn, provides the motivation to connect in ways that permit us to act on our desire to support others.
- To age positively, we need to encourage respect, cooperation, support, and trust for each other. Connections with others can help make this happen if they are established with these positive intentions.
- Finally, bringing elders together to discuss and share ideas can foster a sense of community. However, many of us may lack the skill or ability to reach out and make these important connections without the help of others. Development of

structures and processes, such as those that senior centers offer, support people's ability to connect.

Factors within Ourselves

It's one thing to recognize that life's stages have an internal logic and rhythm that promote growth and development. However, it is quite another thing to have the attitudes and abilities to act on this recognition. If we live long enough and value the importance of connectivity, we have to bring a variety of internal resources to the task of making it happen. Consider the following:

> *It's character that counts.*
> —Louis L' Amour

- One of our most important resources is *our attitude regarding aging*. Do we realistically see ourselves as aging people, or do we try to hold on to the illusion that we are middle-aged or, perhaps, still young? If we accept the fact that we are aging, do we do so with resignation or with anticipation and enthusiasm? It is unlikely that we will invest the energy and time to create and develop the connections that are so important during this advanced life stage if we refuse to accept the fact that we are aging. Even if we do recognize our aging as a reality but do so fatalistically and with sadness, there is little likelihood that we will make the effort to connect positively.

  > *You must grow old ... You'll have to find out what age means, and how to be old ... Whom the gods hate they keep forever young.*
  > —Robertson Davies

  > *Life was meant to be lived, and the curiosity must be kept alive. One must never, for whatever reason, turn his back on life.*
  > —Eleanor Roosevelt

  However, if we are curious and energized by the possibilities that aging holds for us, we are more likely to find the energy and motivation required to pursue, develop, and maintain positive connections.

- Assuming we accept the reality of aging and recognize the importance of being connected with others, it requires *our ability to cope with change* to make it happen. Change requires flexibility, a modicum of risk taking, a nonjudgmental approach to life, and the ability to live with ambiguity. Most of us are like resting rocks that are quite content to stay at rest, probably more than we would like to believe. This is particularly likely to be the case as aging occurs, because it is a time when we become less certain of our status, skills, and abilities. Purposeful efforts have to be initiated to overcome these constraints. Success breeds success: the more we make efforts to forge meaningful relationships, the more we will be able to develop the ability and willingness to extend our connectivity.

> *Happiness is not a state to arrive at, but a manner of traveling.*
> —Margaret Lee Runbeck

- *Our personalities* also affect our ability to develop connective relationships. Reaching out and relating is easy for some but difficult for others, who may need extensive support to make positive connections. For example, those who are *extroverted* in orientation reach out easily and naturally to connect with others. Those who are *introverted* in orientation are less enthused about reaching out and may find doing so to be highly stressful. Similarly, there are those who are *integrated* (high in life satisfactions, mature, open to new experiences, and positive about participating in a variety of activities) and others who are *defensive* (hard-driving but unwilling to come to grips with their aging), and still others who are *passive-dependent* (in need of others to support them or perhaps are even apathetic and engage in very few activities) (Cockerham, 1991). However we look at it, our personalities do impact our interest and ability to form lasting relationships.

> *Seek knowledge of the world and of mankind, and above all, knowledge of ourselves.*
> —Robertson Davies

- Finally, our ability to connect is affected by *our beliefs and behaviors regarding spirituality.* Spiritual people believe that there is an order to the universe and a greater intelligence that guides us. Some may refer to spirituality as God, while others may prefer to think of it in different terms and perhaps with less specific imagery. Regardless of how we define it, the more we are guided by spirituality, the more we are likely to seek connections with others and participate in our communities. Spiritual people believe in the greater order of things and, therefore, are likely to place importance on being connected with others.

> *We ask for long life, but 'tis deep life, or noble moments that signify. Let the measure of time be spiritual, not mechanical.*
> —Ralph Waldo Emerson

> *The spiritual eyesight improves as the physical eyesight declines.*
> —Plato

Environmental Factors

Most of us require support as we grow older, especially to help us reach out and connect with others. The problem is that we live in a rapidly changing world that is becoming more difficult to comprehend. We can't count as much on traditional support systems, such as religious institutions and intergenerational homes. Conscious efforts need to be made to create and sustain positive environments that serve our need for connectivity. Groups, communities, and government agencies that want to help aging people connect positively and effectively need to consider the following:

> *There is nothing permanent except change.*
> —Heraclitus

- Perhaps most important, *a culture of care needs to be promoted.* Difficult as this may appear, given our fast-paced society and the shrinking of close neighborhood and community bonds, we need to pursue this goal for all of us—the young, the middle-aged, and those who are older. A culture of care is not a new idea. In the past, our forbearers found ways to care for older citizens and help them stay connected, and this is still the way things are in many parts of the world. Given today's realities, it will be a major challenge for developed countries, but we can reverse the current trend toward heightened loneliness and isolation if we decide to do so. For example, we can promote new definitions of community based on common interests and needs rather than common spaces; engage in town hall–type dialogues and debates; and broaden the scope of community center activities and attract more people to participate in them. We can also expand efforts to bring people together to live in alternative housing arrangements such as intergenerational housing, shared housing among the elderly, day care, elder care, assisted living, and progressive care situations. Such alternatives are more creative and diverse than the dichotomous choice of remaining in one's own home or living in a nursing home.

- *The impact of media on the ability and willingness of older people to connect needs to be considered.* As noted earlier, there are two dominant and erroneous images portrayed by TV, magazines, newspapers, and movies. One image is of aging people as lonely, irascible, inflexible, behind the times, and incapable of change. The

> *A graceful and honorable old age is the childhood of immorality.*
>
> —Pindar

other image is of older people who try to prolong their middle-aged years by looking younger than their chronological age and refusing to "grow old." Neither of these stereotypical images is accurate. Worse still, they leave us with the conclusion that helping older people to connect is a waste of time. Those who are seen as incapable of change are thought to be beyond help, uninterested, and preferring to be left alone, while those who are seen as youth oriented are presumed to be capable and not in need of any assistance from others. The reality is that most of us are trying to come to terms with aging and have the desire to connect, but we can benefit greatly if the media portrayed images that are more realistic. It would help families, groups, organizations, and governmental agencies to be more focused and realistic in their efforts to help the aging connect positively and effectively.

- *Rituals, norms, and language systems can provide meaningful expectations and guidelines for behavior that should help the aging gain confidence and skills to connect with others positively.* These expectations were simpler and clearer in the past because there were fewer of us, and life changed more slowly than it does today. People lived in smaller communities, stayed put for generations, and learned what was expected of them early in life. Now there are many more of us, the pace of life is much faster, most of us live in large cities, and we move across large distances with ease. The more of us there are, and the easier it is to pack up and resettle elsewhere, the harder it becomes to connect with each other. Given these changes, we need to create new ground rules that promote cooperation rather than competition, teaming rather than isolation, and, above all, support and trust. We need to create rituals, norms, expectations, and language systems that bind us together effectively and help us know what is expected of us as we move through life's stages. We also need new definitions and forms of community, based on common interests rather than proximity. These are all important tasks. They will require time for discussion, debate, and consensus building. The more widespread the involvement, the more likely it is that we will develop meaningful responses.
- *We need to promote strategies that bring people together.* These include strategies that are intergenerational based (e.g., mentoring programs); family based (e.g., rituals and celebrations that focus on life's passages); religious organization membership based (e.g., study groups and religious school teaching); and community based (e.g., participating in senior center activities). The more options that exist, the more likely it is that aging people will be able to find some meaningful ways of connecting. Continuing efforts also need to be made to make more information available so elders can be aware of the

> *If a family has an old person in it, it possesses a jewel.*
> —Chinese proverb

options that are available to connect with each other in positive ways. For instance, governmental and private sector directories of agencies that promote bringing older people together can be published and distributed widely to those at this life stage.

- *Learning communities, based on adult learning principles, can be made widely available to older people,* most of whom are interested in learning and have the time available to do so. Organizations like Elderhostel, as well as universities and adult education programs at the local level, have attracted large numbers of aging people. There are even residential housing arrangements on more than a hundred university campuses, developed to promote older learning communities. Age is no barrier to learning, but the unique needs and interests of older learners need to be taken into consideration. The principles of adult learning, wherein learners plays a major role in selecting the subject matter and are consulted about how it is delivered, must also be considered.

- *Living situations that promote meaning, continuity, pride, and security can increase the opportunity for older people to connect.* This may appear to be obvious, but it can't be taken for granted in a society that is intent on developing an ever-increasing number of depersonalized institutional settings to house its senior citizens, and in which, for the first time in history, more people die in hospitals than at home in their own beds. We recognize the importance of providing good living situations when we raise our families, but we don't seem to recognize that we also need to remain in our own homes as older people. These are settings that represent independence, where so many memories were made and where we are close to friends and families who care about us. They are also located in communities we are familiar with and care about. With adequate access to public programs and public spaces, the benefits of having aging people stay in their own homes are extensive. We need to rethink our tendency to warehouse older people in institutions, whether for seemingly positive reasons or for reasons of convenience and ease. If

> There is somebody wiser than any of us, and that is everybody.
> —Napoleon

people are unable to manage living in their own homes, we need to find other alternatives for them. For example, they can be encouraged to join together and share roles and responsibilities in ways that enable them to remain independent in their own homes or in other shared housing situations. The combination of security, pride, and stimulation that can be fostered is extremely important. Older people can live in such alternative housing situations even if they are not fully independent. Meals on Wheels and home health-care services may be more than sufficient to meet their needs without having to live in nursing homes.

- *Interdependence needs to be promoted over codependence or independence. Codependence* is about needing others to feel complete. It is a term that refers to relationships in which individuals are not self-sufficient. They require others to provide things for them that they can't, or at least think they can't, provide for themselves. *Independence*, on the contrary, is about focusing on self-sufficiency and minimizing mutually supportive relations with others because we believe they might lead to making commitments we would rather not make. *Interdependence* is about being capable of taking care of yourself but recognizing that there is great value in connecting with others. Interdependent people know that in the give-and-take of supporting others and being supported by them, they can be even stronger. They can ask for and accept help if they need it, as well as volunteer and give help when others might benefit from their support. Since neither codependence nor independence is likely to form an adequate foundation for connectivity and mutuality, it makes sense to develop structures and processes that promote the benefits of interdependence.

> ## Exercise: You and Connectivity
>
> This activity is intended to help you summarize your understanding of connectivity.
>
> 1. Why do you want to connect with others? List the most important reasons:
>
> A.
> B.
> C.
> D.
> E.
>
> 2. Did you have difficulty identifying five reasons? Can you identify more?
> 3. Do you need to think more about the meaning and value of your connections?
> 4. Are you doing anything to help others who are in need of enriching their own connections? Can you do more to be of help to others?

In Closing

We began the chapter by reading about Sam, who was concerned that his connections were thinning out. Many of the caring people in his life were no longer available because of death, geographical dispersal, or infirmities, and his old community connections weren't of much interest to him. He was feeling alone and lonely.

He knew that he would have to reach out to develop positive connections, and that he would have to guard against becoming negative and cynical about the future. However, his pain and anguish could also serve as an energy source to get moving and engaged.

He reflected about connections that had given him pleasure and satisfaction earlier in life. For example, even though he initially was not inclined to reconnect with schools in the community, he recalled how much he enjoyed participating in his children's schools and decided to volunteer to do so again. He began by assisting teachers at the local elementary school, where volunteers were needed to work with children to improve their reading skills. After doing this for a while, he concluded that many children need more love and care, especially children who come from broken families, do not have grandparents, or whose grandparents are not available to them on a regular basis. It wasn't long before he became a surrogate grandfather for some of these children.

He also focused on establishing new connections with people his own age. He discovered that becoming involved in activities at the local senior center was a good way of finding people who shared similar interests and concerns. In addition, he took some personal development courses through continuing education at a local university. These courses motivated him to pursue his interest in photography and gardening. They also provided a means to connect with others who shared these interests. As he gained confidence, he expanded his efforts to connect. He became more active in his church and volunteered to assist at services. This gave him a great deal of satisfaction, a feeling that he belonged and that he was of value.

As he became more comfortable about connecting with others, he decided that he didn't want to live alone. After much thought, he opened his home to others who wanted to live in a cooperative housing situation. It was not long before Sam began to look forward to life with enthusiasm. He felt enthused about the future.

Chapter Four

Clear, Consistent, and Appropriate Boundaries

Man arrives as a novice at each age of his [or her] life.
—Sebastian-Roch Nicolas de Chamfort

Sally was perplexed. The ground rules she'd followed to lead her life seemed to have lost their relevance. Until recently, there were clear rules and beliefs that guided her busy life. When she was growing up, her parents made rules and set boundaries on her behaviors. After she married and became a full-time mom, she negotiated expectations with her spouse and got lots of guidance from Dr. Spock, as well as endless advice from family members about how to be a mother and raise children. After her kids left home and her husband died, she got her teaching credentials and spent more than twenty years as an elementary teacher, where she was guided by government regulations, school system policies, school administrator expectations, and her own expanding repertoire of effective classroom management techniques.

She was proud of her achievements and was sure she would manage her older years just fine. However, soon after she retired, she realized that the imposed and self-developed boundaries that had guided her through her earlier life stages were not appropriate for this new stage of her life. Worse still, there were no obvious guidelines that she could identify to replace them, no clear set of boundary expectations for her older years. Not surprisingly, she was beginning to feel confused. How should she behave? What did others expect of her? What should her own behavioral rules and boundaries be? She felt the need to find answers to these questions because she wanted to feel more secure about who she was becoming and how she might live her elder years effectively and meaningfully.

Sally was transitioning from a life stage that was familiar and comfortable into one that was not at all clear to her. She felt like a stranger in a strange new land, without an adequate guidebook to help her understand the language or the terrain. She knew she would have to figure out how to conduct her life, but what were the expectations? She thought there must be laws, policies, and rules that could help define limits and expectations. She also thought there must be norms and cultural expectations, those implicit but powerful boundary definers developed over time by informal groups, organizations, communities, and society. What were the beliefs about how things should and should not be done in her aging years? During the earlier phases of her life—childhood and adolescence, young adulthood, marriage and motherhood, and during her career as a long-time teacher—Sally was clear about both codified and implicit boundary expectations. She accepted and lived by them because they provided structure and meaning for her life. Now she could no longer count on them to guide her life, and she had little idea about what might replace them.

This is a challenging experience, one that we all have to come to terms with when we cross over into our retirement years. In this chapter, we will first examine what we mean when we talk about boundaries that can guide our older years. Second, we will explore obstacles that we need to overcome in order to clarify and adapt appropriate boundaries that can help us function effectively. Third, we will discuss the importance of our own perspectives and attitudes, and how they affect our beliefs about boundaries, as well as our thinking about the problems and potentials of our aging years. Finally, we will review strategies that can help us and those who support us—family members, friends, community organizations, and others—develop, establish, and maintain effective boundary expectations for our aging years.

Why We Need Clear, Consistent and Appropriate Boundaries to Guide Us in Our Older Years

Most of us, especially in the Western world, tend to think of boundaries as limitations and barriers. We bristle at the thought of having limitations and barriers placed on our behaviors, but the fact is that without boundaries, we feel lost and unclear about how to conduct our lives. Appropriate, meaningful, and equitable boundaries help us feel secure, safe, and under control.

Boundaries also provide the foundation for our growth and development as human beings. They help us feel secure enough to take the risks that are necessary to connect with others, learn relevant life skills, receive support and care, move toward high expectations for our own growth, and engage in meaningful activities.

> *The art of progress is to preserve order amid change and preserve change amid order.*
> —Alfred North Whitehead

If boundaries are based on rigid and inflexible rules that limit expectations for our behaviors, we will likely feel constrained and controlled. If they are vague, they won't provide sufficient guidance, and we may not know what behaviors are appropriate. Either way, we are likely to become confused, fearful, and insecure. Clear and appropriate boundaries are important because they allow us to establish and maintain quality lives, so we need to draw our boundaries carefully.

> *Nothing will ever be attempted if all possible objections must be first overcome.*
> —William James

Boundaries are important at all life stages. Those for children, adolescents, young adults, and the middle-aged are well established, and sanctions for not abiding by them are fairly clear. We have done a pretty good job of codifying expectations at these earlier life stages, but so far we have not done as well for the post-retirement life stage. Boundaries for those in retirement and beyond are not well delineated or agreed upon, and the sanctions are not at all clear. In part, this may be due to the negative mythologies that were discussed earlier. But it is also related to the fact that it is only recently that so many of us have survived long enough to populate this older life stage.

> *Our task is to listen to the news that is always arriving out of silence.*
> —Rilke

Mike M. Milstein

Why Is It So Difficult to Develop Clear Boundaries for Aging?

Most of us place increasing importance on the effective use of the limited time remaining for us as we age. We need to be clear about the rules of the game if we are going to put our energies into living meaningful and fulfilling lives. We need a sufficient comfort level and a sense of place to get on with the things that matter most to us during our aging years.

> *Joyous distrust is a sign of health. Everything absolute belongs to pathology.*
> —Fredrich Nietzche

The media makes it difficult to establish new and meaningful boundaries to guide our aging lives, mainly because of two stereotypical, contradictory, and inaccurate images that it perpetuates regarding older people. One image is that aging people need to rest, disengage from societal responsibilities, and slide gradually into decline, dementia, and death. This image is far from reality. In fact, most of us manage to retain a modicum of physical health and active lifestyles during our aging years. The other image is of silver-haired, bright-eyed, physically healthy, and highly engaged elders who tenaciously hang on to earlier life stages. This image is a fleeting reality for only a small minority of aging people who try to hold on to their former lives as long as possible. Staying physically fit is important, but it should not require that we deny the realities of aging. Doing so is a losing game that can cause us to delay experiencing the opportunities and challenges that await us in our older years.

Both of these media-created aging portraits constrain our development. What we need are realistic images about the new life space we are arriving at in our life's journey. We are in need of guidance about how to make the most out of our new reality. For example, we need to do the following:

- let go of old roles and expectations so we can move through this challenging transition and grow into our older selves
- focus on developing goals, priorities, and a course of action to guide the use of our time and activities

- learn how to relate, remain connected, obtain support from and contribute to those around us
- be aware of expectations of others about our behaviors, and be clear about how we want to respond to them
- Take the necessary risks to reflect about and establish our own internally driven boundary preferences
- realize that we will probably reinvent ourselves more than once as we move through our older years
- develop the flexibility and ability to redefine our boundaries as necessary
- live with integrity and be true to ourselves

> *It is not length of life, but depth of life.*
> —Ralph Waldo Emerson

The changing demographics of the older population have increased the urgency to sort through boundary complexities and confusions regarding our aging years. More of us are living longer and staying healthier. Many in this age group also have more disposable income and are intent on growing and developing. The predominant images we hold of poverty and decline among the aging are not realistic for the majority of older people.

Most of us want more clarity about expectations and boundaries so we can focus on the task of living well. The first step in establishing effective boundaries is to identify the core issues involved, confront critical blockages, and clear up confusions that keep us from developing effective rules and expectations for aging. The four issues noted below are particularly relevant.

Society's Images

We are surrounded by false and negative images of aging. These images make it difficult to establish positive boundaries. High on the list of these detrimental images are:

- *We are old when we become sixty-five.* This may be the start of old age for some, but it certainly is not the reality for those of us who choose to

> *The nicest thing about growing old is you don't have to worry about it anymore.*
> —George Burns

stay active, whether through participating in full-time or part-time employment, engaging in voluntary activities, or exploring and pursuing other creative life activities.
- *Retirement means retiring or disengaging from society.* This is the furthest thing from most older people's minds. In fact, for most people, retirement provides opportunities to pursue their interests more fully than at earlier times in life. Family obligations and career pursuits are usually behind for most of us. There are increasing opportunities to move on and explore aspects of ourselves that we were too busy to examine earlier in life.

> *I don't long for the good old days. I'm too busy trying to create some good new days.*
> —Gene Perret

- *Most older people will have to cope with dementia and are likely to be institutionalized.* Nothing is further from the truth. As noted, a small percentage of the elderly are institutionalized, with the average age of institutionalization being about eighty. The same low percentages apply to those coping with Alzheimer's disease. For the rest of us, as depicted in Chapter 2, there is growing evidence that our physical health will remain relatively robust until shortly before we die, rather than slide rapidly downward toward disability early in our aging years.

Loss of the Known

Many of us arrive at our aging years with little preparation, especially if we retire after many years in well-defined work-related roles. Relatively few employers provide pre-retirement counseling, and those that do usually focus on economic issues such as estimates of retirement income, budgeting strategies, health benefits, and taxes. Few provide counseling about quality-of-life issues such as transitioning from one's role in the workplace into retirement or developing goals and activities to replace those that guided us during our working lives. Without such counseling, our early retirement years can be challenging. Many aging people who have gone through this transition period refer to it in the following ways:

- Like our adolescent years, when we experienced many physical changes and had little sense of control over our lives.
- As a time of loss. Priority goals and activities that were central to one's life earlier are likely to become less meaningful. This is especially true for those who held high-status positions, because the gap between the well-understood past and the unstructured present will probably be greater for them than others.
- Confusing at best and frightening at worst. Known boundaries evaporate and new ones are not yet clear. There is a realization that along with fewer restrictions and obligations, there is also less clarity of expectations.
- A feeling of aimlessness, of not knowing what to do with our newfound freedom and the time that has become available to us.

Medical Advances

The rapid rate of discovery and improvement in the medical world has changed the physical realities of aging. Better diagnostic tools, technological developments, and more sophisticated treatment techniques mean that more of us will remain healthier and live longer than any generation that came before us. However, there are challenges associated with these changes:

> *We have inadvertently trained our young doctors to consider it a virtue to prolong life for the sole purpose of prolonging it.*
> —James Howard Means

- The medical world continues to try to *cure* older people of disease, when what most of us really need is *management* of chronic conditions. The emphasis on curing is expensive and is not usually realistic anyway. Most of us are capable of adjusting to chronic medical conditions and are more interested in putting our energies into living as fully as possible.
- As noted, largely due to medical advances, there has been about a decade gain in our physical and mental abilities (Sheehy 1995). However, social and psychological changes in expectations,

structures, and boundaries have not kept pace. We are only now coming to grips with the meaning of these added years of well-being.

Coming to Terms with Our Mortality

We live in a culture that attempts to deny the existence of death. We even buffer ourselves from death by delegating a small group of professionals—doctors, nurses, funeral home directors, and morticians—to relieve us of the responsibility of having to deal with the death of loved ones on a firsthand basis. It is as though by not recognizing death's existence, we believe it can't happen to us. Besides being naive, denial limits our ability to age well. We need to realize that per Shachter-Shalomi and Miller (1995, p.81), "Death is not a cosmic mistake ... The presence of death deepens our appreciation of life. It also regenerates our psyches in preparation for harvesting."

> *Fear of death is worse than death itself.*
> —Proverb

> *Both life and death are parts of the same great adventure.*
> —Theodore Roosevelt

Death is our ultimate boundary: the more we are in touch with the reality of our mortality, the more likely it is that we will lead purposeful lives. As we move through our aging years, we have to decide how we will deal with the inevitability of our own deaths. Those who come to terms with mortality and accept death as a part of life's experience are likely to put legal and financial affairs in order, write living wills, and give thought to what it will be like to experience dying. If we understand that our time is finite and recognize that death is a meaningful part of our life experience, we are more likely to live each day fully and meaningfully.

> *The death rate remains constant and total, as it has since the dawn of time.*
> —Dr. Gernst Biladi

> *To everything there is a season, and a time to every purpose under the heaven: a time to be born, and a time to die; a time to plant and a time to pluck up that which is planted...*
> —Ecclesiastes

Those of us who are unwilling to

cope with the implications of death tenaciously avoid reflecting about this reality. But if we are not prepared to come to terms with our mortality, we may become stuck and rigid in our ways and miss an extraordinary opportunity to synthesize life's experiences. As a result, we are also more likely to live in fear rather than fully embrace our older years.

In *A Year to Live* (1997), Stephen Levine, who is a major guide concerning dying and death, describes how he chose to live a year of his life as though it was his last. Focusing on his own death, he found that the intensity of each moment was heightened. In fact, this intensity about life remained high long after the prescribed year was over. His experience supports the belief that if we hope to live our days fully, we must confront the reality of our death.

DEALING WITH BOUNDARIES: IT'S ALL ABOUT YOUR PERSPECTIVE

We know that the number of people in their sixties and beyond is increasing rapidly. What we don't know is the extent to which the aging years of the current group of elders, as well as the boomer generation and others who are following, will be qualitatively different from the aging lives of earlier generations.

Why do some people act and feel old in their fifties or sixties, while others remain energized and engaged with creativity and enthusiasm in their eighties and nineties? The difference has a lot to do with how people perceive aging and how they choose to define themselves. Those who rapidly age mentally and physically tend to see the glass as half-empty. Those who do so more slowly and with more energy tend to see the glass as half-full.

> *Be careful how you interpret the world; it is like that.*
> —Joseph Heller

The Half-Empty Glass Perspective

Those who are guided by half-empty glass perceptions see aging as a time of decline and diminishment. They are likely to:
- live within rigid and constraining boundaries

- avoid thinking about aging because they think it won't be a positive experience
- believe that their aging years will be marked by ever-decreasing ability to control their lives
- believe that aging people and the communities they live in will gradually but inevitably withdraw from each other
- With such attitudes, growing older can indeed come to look like our worst fear. Carried to its logical extreme, they can lead to the development of constricting and limiting boundaries as well as a sense of helplessness and increasing physical and emotional illness.

> *Gratitude is riches. Complaining is poverty. Instead of complaining about what's wrong, be grateful for what's right.*
> —Zachery Fisher

> *We cannot help the birds of sadness flying over our heads, but we need not let them build nests in our hair.*
> —Chinese saying

The Half-Full Glass Perspective

Those who are guided by half-full glass perceptions see aging as a time of potential, a time to develop flexible and expansive boundaries. If we take this approach, we will probably see our older years as a time of growth and development, when the following occurs:

- Life opens up with increasing possibilities.
- Life has fewer constraints, requirements, and expectations as career and family responsibilities dwindle or disappear, and there are more opportuni-

> *A new kind of security and confidence is felt—a confidence that does not need guarantees, that is based simply on our growing inner experience.*
> —Fritz Kunkel and Roy E. Dickerson

ties to express ourselves as we choose than at any previous life stage.
- Energy and attention can be focused on new priorities or harnessed to delve deeper into priorities that could not be fully developed earlier in life.
- Growing older means just that, *growing*.
- There are opportunities to be creative.
- We can continue to engage fully in life.
- We can synthesize life's experiences and accumulate sufficient wisdom to make meaningful contributions to our families, friends, and communities.

In short, our attitudes make a big difference in how we live our aging years. Depending on our perspectives, we will choose to engage or disengage with life in our older years. Fortunately, many of us are choosing to maintain a high level of activity rather than fixate on the inevitability of aging, decline, and death.

> *For age is opportunity no less than youth itself, tho' in another dress and as the evening twilight fades away the sky is filled with stars invisible by day.*
> —Henry Wadsworth Longfellow

> **Exercise: What You See Is What You Get**
>
> What is your predominant orientation—engaging or disengaging? The following exercise is intended to help you clarify which orientation describes you most accurately.
>
> 1. In your community, you probably have observed aging people who have chosen to disengage. Think about some specific ways you have seen them disengage. List some examples that stand out for you.
>   A.
>   B.
>   C.
>   D.
> 2. Why do you think they chose to disengage? List a few reasons.
>   A.
>   B.
>   C.
>   D.
> 3. How do you see yourself? Are you more like those who disengage, or are you more like those who have found ways of staying engaged? What does this tell you about yourself?
> 4. What needs to be changed so that aging people do not feel that they have to disengage? What would it take for this to happen?

Promoting Clear, Consistent, and Appropriate Boundaries

We know that we need meaningful boundaries to live well. We also know that as we pass through younger life stages and transition into our older years, the boundaries that had earlier provided structure and guidance probably will no longer suffice. We also know that new boundaries are not easy to identify. Given the importance of establishing and maintaining clear, consistent, and appropriate boundaries, especially at this stage of life, when there is so little clarity about expectations, we need to focus on them actively and creatively.

There are things that we can do to develop and maintain healthy boundaries. There are also things that others—family members, friends, caregivers, and community-based organizations—can do for us in order to support our need for effective boundaries. The strategies presented below are not inclusive, but they provide a solid starting point that can be extended as needed.

What We Can Do

If we wait for others to define our boundaries, we give them control over our lives, which is not a positive way to develop a meaningful and internally driven life. Equally important, if we leave this task to others, we will become passive participants, dependent upon the beliefs and preferences of others. There

> *Not everyone's life is what they make it. Some people's life is what other people make of it.*
> —Alice Walker

is much we can do for ourselves to carve out meaningful boundaries. For example, we can:

- **Come to terms with aging.** This is an important starting place. As noted, holding on to images of ourselves from earlier life stages, when the reality is that we have moved on chronologically, emotionally, and physically, is a losing battle. More important, it delays us from laying a foundation for our aging years. The other extreme, viewing aging as nothing more than a prelude to death, is also dysfunctional. This can lead us to accept our lot fatalistically and do little or nothing to develop meaningful guidelines for our older years. We need

> *Age is a question of mind over matter. If you don't mind, it doesn't matter.*
> —Satchel Page

> *A man is always startled when he hears himself seriously called an old man for the first time.*
> —O. W. Holmes, Sr.

to accept our aging as a fact of life and get on with creating boundaries that help us deal with it effectively. Fixating on and over-glorifying the past or dreading the future saps the energy we need to live in the present and to plan for the future. We need to develop an honest, clear, and accurate picture of ourselves. How do we want to live our lives? What are our goals and priorities? How are we preparing to live for the foreseeable future? These are important questions. Reflecting about them can move us from *doing*, which predominated at earlier life stages, to *being*, which focuses on spirituality and wisdom building, both of which are increasingly important for most aging people.

- **Reduce reliance on ego**. On the plus side, our egos are powerful engines that help us navigate life. They provide the energy we need to compete and accomplish. They also support the development of our self-esteem and our self-confidence. However, while the ego is an important asset during earlier life stages, it can become a major deficit that we have to learn how to hold in check during our aging years. First, reducing reliance on our egos is an important step toward clarification and development of boundaries to guide our lives. Second, if we are able to set our egos aside, we can let go of past roles and behaviors, and we are in a better position to transition into our older years. Third, holding our egos in check also helps us let go of being the experts we spent years becoming during earlier life stages and turn our focus on being amateurs—novices who can be playful learners because we aren't expected to have all the answers. Being amateurs is a worthwhile experience because it enriches our potential to grow and develop at this advanced stage of life. Finally, hanging on tenaciously to ego also inhibits our spiritual development in later life. Our egos focus our attention on what we know and do well, whereas development of spirituality

> *The fatal metaphor of progress, which means leaving things behind us, has utterly obscured the real idea of growth, which means leaving things inside us.*
> —G. K. Chesterton

focuses our attention on exploring our connection to the universe and on our belief and faith in a greater power, a power that is unknowable.

- **Create and maintain a good quality of life.** Meaningful boundaries and expectations can enhance the quality of our lives if we start with the attitude that our older years also bring unique opportunities. But we need to create our own expansive boundaries if we hope to achieve our potential for growth and development. Rather than retire to the rocking chair, we need to challenge ourselves. For example, society may send signals that we are bound to lose mental flexibility and that our sexuality will diminish, but this does not have to be our reality if we create boundaries and expectations that promote our continuing growth and development. The old saw "Use it or lose it" rings true. For example, we need to stimulate our brains to keep them nimble, as well as maintain a level of sexual activity that is appropriate and satisfying.

> *The greatest discovery of my generation is that a human being can change his life by changing his attitude of mind.*
> —William James

- **Exercise the right to make decisions.** Prior to our aging years, we spent most of our lives making our own decisions. As children and adolescents, we chafed when we were constrained from managing our lives. We enjoyed the expanded opportunities to manage our own lives as young adults and assumed the right to make decisions for ourselves and our children as we moved through our thirties and forties. We cherished the empty-nest freedoms we got when our kids left home. Then, after all these years of expanding freedom to make decisions, according to a predominate societal image, we are supposed to become passive participants in our own lives, letting others, such as family, government, and organizations

> *You only live once, but if you work it right, once is enough.*
> —Joe E. Lewis

that care for us make many of our decisions. We need to be wary of letting this happen, even if it is for the best of intentions. We need to make decisions about our lives or externally imposed boundaries will be drawn ever tighter around us, leaving us little room or ability to take charge of our lives.

- **Prepare for the aging years before retiring.** We can start to develop structures and rules of behavior that we want to put in place long before we reach our aging years. The sooner we start thinking about and planning for what we want our older life to look like, the more likely it is that we will actually have that kind of experience. However, doing

> *To know how to grow old is the master work of wisdom, and one of the most difficult chapters in the great art of living.*
> —Henri Frederic Amiel

so requires the ability to seek information, as well as to listen, observe, and learn from those who have already wrestled with these issues and have entered their aging years. The gains to be had more than justify the efforts required.

Support by Others

We also need the support of governmental and nongovernmental groups and organizations to help us create and maintain effective boundaries. This support can come in a variety of forms. For example:

- **Invite members of the aging population to participate in the development and modification of policies, rules, and regulations that affect them**. Local and national governments develop policies, rules, and regulations that establish boundaries for acceptable behaviors. Various private organizations also develop policies, rules and regulations that affect us. These include, for example, health maintenance organizations, hospitals, and community-based organizations such as senior centers. The policies, rules, and regulations that are promulgated can support our growth and development, or they can be obtrusive and impinge upon the quality of our lives. If policies, rules, and regulations regarding older people are based on the assumption that aging is a time of disengagement, decline, and death, older people will be placed at a disadvantage. This is more likely to be the case if others who are younger and have little firsthand knowledge about the realities of growing older formulate them. It is hard enough to figure out our boundaries without having to cope with negative and contradictory policies, rules, and regulations. Many policies and rules are created without the benefit of adequate research, let alone meaningful feedback from elders. We need to engage aging people in the process before final decisions are made because they know what they need, and they have to live with the policies and rules that affect them. They can participate as members of planning groups and advisory committees. They can also be asked to respond to surveys that seek information about how older people think and feel about things. Such involvement can increase the likelihood that policies and rules will be clear and appropriate for those they affect. Finally, we need to make sure that they are communicated clearly and frequently. They also need to be disseminated as widely as possible so that those who are affected will get the information they need without having to make extraordinary efforts to do so.

> *Those self-appointed experts on old age know the literature but not the life.*
> —Malcom Cowley

- **Help aging people stay in control of their own lives.** Whether living autonomously, in cooperative arrangements with others, in assisted living situations, or even in nursing homes, most of us want to be in control of our own lives. We want to make our own choices regarding the management of daily living and, if needed, about the care we receive. For this to happen, we need consistent and meaningful support from family members, friends,

> *When an individual is kept in a situation of inferiority, the fact is that he does become inferior.*
> —Simone de Beauvoir

community organizations, and governmental agencies. If we are pressed by others to accept their judgments and decisions and we do not get support for our own preferences, we will probably become frustrated and conclude that we will have little control over our lives. In fact, we might experience learned helplessness, the perceived inability to take actions required to meet our needs, which is likely to happen when we believe that others control our lives.

- **Promote alternative arrangements that support independent living.** Most older people prefer to live in their own homes, at least until it becomes too difficult to continue to do so. Others seek alternative arrangements, including sharing homes or living in planned communities. Few voluntarily choose to live in institutions such as nursing homes primarily because they perceive that such living situations would make it difficult for them to maintain their autonomy and self-control. In other words, we seek out living situations in which we can set our own boundaries and resist situations that are likely to compromise our ability to do so. Knowing this, it is important that family members, government agencies, and others involved in making decisions about housing arrangements for older people, do all they can to support autonomous living choices for as long as it is feasible.

- **Create rituals and rites of passage that promote meaningfulness in our aging years.** So-called primitive societies invest significant efforts in the development of rituals and rites of passages for all life stages, including moving from youth to young adulthood, leaving the home of origin, mating and childbearing, economic independence, and, finally, the challenges and accomplishments of our older years, including growing spiritually and sharing our wisdom. Most so-called developed nations don't do enough to promote these important life's passages demarcations. We need to practice existing rituals and rites of passages and supplement them with new ones, particularly for our older population. In particular, we need to celebrate the transition from the world of work to retirement and then the move through the challenges of our older years.

Rituals and rites of passages can send clear signals to aging people about desired behaviors. For example, we need to recognize achievements in post-retirement years and give due recognition to contributions that are voluntary and without pay. These contributions are every bit as meaningful as earlier achievements, which are usually viewed as more important because they are associated with earning power. We also need to promote and support elders' efforts to synthesize their lives and share the wisdom that they can bring to a world that can well benefit from such guidance.

Exercise: You and Clear, Consistent and Boundaries

This brief activity is intended to help you summarize your understanding about boundary preferences.

1. List the five most important rules (e.g., the ability to make my own decisions; opportunities for growth and development) that are foundational building blocks for your boundaries.
2.
   A.
   B.
   C.
   D.
   E.
3. Did you have difficulty identifying five? Could you have identified more?
4. Do you need to give more thought to establishing preferences and expectations regarding your aging boundaries?
5. Do you provide help to others who are in need of establishing their aging boundaries? Can you do more to help others?

Mike M. Milstein

In Closing

At the outset of Chapter 4, a brief vignette was presented about Sally and her need to establish viable boundaries. She was confused. The rules that provided meaningful boundaries for her in the past weren't proving to be helpful as guides for living in her older years. Neither were the old rule makers—her parents, husband, work supervisors, and others. She knew that she needed to take responsibility for developing boundaries that would give her a sense of security and predictability. Without them, she would continue to feel anxious and unsure of how to conduct her life. She concluded that she would have to focus on boundaries that would be positive and relevant, both now and in the future, and that they would have to promote a balance between safety on one side and growth and development on the other side.

The first thing she did was think about what she would have to let go of to be able to age well, including known rules that were no longer helpful. She also knew that she had to get clear about the reality of her own aging. She started to pay closer attention to society's pervasive messages about staying young as long as possible and told herself she could not be taken in by them if she hoped to create a meaningful life for her older years.

Sally started thinking about older family members and friends who could be good role models for aging positively and, with a bit of coaxing, might even agree to serve as mentors. She sought out people she respected who were further along in their aging years, hoping they might be able to help her develop meaningful boundaries to guide her life. She was pleased to find that people responded positively and enthusiastically, especially a favorite aunt and an old friend, both of whom signed on as mentors and were soon sharing important insights with her.

Sally also visited the local library to find reading material that could provide guidance for people who are interested in effective aging. Her reading led her to the conclusion that she needed to come to terms with the fact of her aging and her mortality if she expected to live fully. She also picked up some ideas about developing rituals and celebrations, and she started to reward herself with tickets to the local symphony orchestra and to the theater. She also reached out by volunteering her time and talents in community planning initiatives for older citizens.

Most important, she came to the realization that she had to make her own decisions about boundaries to guide her life. She took time to reflect about this, looking inward for her choices so she could be in control of her own life.

Chapter Five
Life-Guiding Skills

The man [or woman] who is too old to learn was probably always too old to learn.

—Henry S. Haskins

Bill recently retired from a corporate executive position. People in his company had relied on him for leadership, conflict management, and problem solving, especially when things really got tough. He always came through in the pinch, and subordinates, peers, and bosses recognized him as an important asset to the organization.

Now here he was, with all these proven leadership skills, ready to enjoy his "golden years." Instead, he quickly came to feel like an amateur in this new world called retirement. It seemed as if nothing he'd learned in order to help him perform his job so well had prepared him for his new life. In fact, he began to think that his experiences might even have made it more difficult for him to make the transition. His expertise was no longer in demand, and his past organizational status no longer had any relevance. He had so much to learn about life after retirement. How was he going to let go of the past so he could develop attitudes and behaviors that would serve him well at this new and challenging life stage? How was he supposed to interact with others? How was he going to re-create meaning in this new land?

Bill had left a well-known world behind, one that rewarded him in a variety of ways, including a good income, authority, and high status. He now found himself washed ashore in a new world that was not familiar—and among people who didn't seem to be terribly impressed or even interested in his past accomplishments.

What Bill was experiencing is not at all unusual, particularly for people who occupied high-status and responsible positions during their working years. The skills that he had honed so well might still be helpful, but they would need to be modified to fit his new situation. There are also other life-guiding skills that he may not have viewed as relevant earlier in life that he needed to learn.

In essence, after decades of being an "expert," Bill had become an "amateur" again. He had much to learn about his new life situation, as well as how to meet its challenges. Retirement can be wonderful, but it also brings new and unique challenges. Retired people often talk about their first post-working years as a time of confusion, frustration, and loss. It is a significant transition. Behaviors that may no longer be useful need to be modified or even stripped away, and new behaviors that may be a better fit at this life stage need to be developed.

For most of us, it will take some time to adapt and change. After all, it took years to learn the behaviors and skills that served us well in earlier life stages. Why should we expect it to be any different when we move into our aging years, especially given the lack of clear-cut expectations to guide us through this stage of life?

Chapter 5 explores life-guiding skills that are necessary to lead meaningful and positive aging lives. We begin with a brief review of important life-guiding skills and then present strategies that can help us in our efforts to develop and practice them effectively.

THE IMPORTANCE OF LIFE-GUIDING SKILLS

Life-guiding skills can help us respond more effectively to the challenges that come our way. Most of us readily recognize the importance of goal setting, planning, communications, decision making, problem solving, and conflict management and resolution. We learn these skills and improve our ability to practice them over time, but they need to be reconsidered, modified, and sharpened as we move from one stage of life to another, especially as we grow older. These life-guiding skills, which are summarized below, are also stepping-stones toward the development of other important capabilities that become more important as we age, including mentoring, spirituality, and wisdom sharing.

> *The man who has ceased to learn ought not to be allowed to wander around loose in these dangerous days.*
> —M. M. Cody

Planning and Goal Setting. Even knowing that life may have other things in mind for us, setting goals helps us envision preferred futures. Without some sense of where we are going, we are left to drift aimlessly, or we even begin to see our lives through a rearview mirror. What does quality of life mean during your older years? What does it look like? How does it feel? Can you describe it? It's not necessary, or perhaps even appropriate, that your goals are highly specific, but they should be clear enough to provide guidance and important enough to motivate you to act on them.

Problem Solving and Decision Making. Having a vision, setting goals, and making plans are the first steps. To actualize our goals, we need to be able to solve problems and make decisions. This entails clarifying problems or barriers that need to be dealt with; gathering and sorting through information; identifying possible alternative responses; selecting among preferences; making decisions and putting them into practice; monitoring results; making modifications that might be required; and evaluating outcomes. The better we are at doing these things, the more likely it is that we will achieve our goals. For those who have not given much thought to or practiced these skills, this may require learning techniques and developing the discipline required to solve problems and make decisions. For example, we need to break such habits as starting the process too late, not gathering needed information, and making hasty and premature choices among possible solutions.

> *Without problems there would be no possibility of triumph.*
> —Anonymous

Communications. To achieve our goals, we need to be able to make our preferences known, especially when we hope to enlist the help of others to do so. This requires that we become skilled at basic communications skills that promote understanding and support. For example, we need to listen carefully and fully so we can figure out what others are thinking and feeling; ask questions and paraphrase what others say to us so we can be clear about what is being said; describe behaviors—ours and theirs; and share our thinking and feelings so others can know what's motivating us. The more we practice these skills, the better we become in applying them, and the more likely we are to receive the support we need to achieve our goals.

Assertiveness and Conflict Management. As we clarify our goals and initiate actions to achieve them, we may encounter resistance and conflict. For example, our families may have different ideas about how we should be living, community agencies may not be able to respond to our needs, and friends may question our choices. We need to learn how to be assertive about our preferences and how to respond to such potentially conflictual situations in ways that promote understanding, cooperation, and support. When conflicts are managed effectively, they can be resolved or at least reduced in intensity. Basic conflict management techniques include clearing up confusion about the meaning of the words we use; sharing full and clear information with everyone involved; and explaining our reasoning processes so others know how we have come to our conclusions. Of course, there will be times when people understand our reasoning but don't agree with it. When this happens, we need to find ways of honoring each other's position, or at least agree to disagree about our differences.

> *Obstacles are those frightful things you see when you take your eyes off your goals.*
> — Henry Ford

The importance of effective life-guiding skills can't be overemphasized, especially given the fact that, on average, more of us are living longer than people did in the past, and that for those who do live longer, the majority will remain healthy, develop new connections, and participate in creative activities for most of these years. Aging myths lead us to believe that most older people decline and move, with varying speed, toward their deaths. However, as we know, the reality is quite different. Relatively few older people end up in nursing homes. Most choose to live on their own and manage to do so quite well for most of their older years, remaining relatively healthy until their final days. Some take advantage of extended years to help their children and grandchildren, give freely of their time and knowledge in community-based volunteer work, and pursue interests and creative activities that may have been set-aside earlier in life or others that are newly developed.

> *The slogan "press on" has solved and always will solve the problems of the human race.*
> —Attributed to Calvin Coolidge

How do so many older people live so well for so long? In part, it's because they learn and develop relevant life-guiding skills. Those who don't are likely to fulfill the images that society has perpetrated: i.e., they are more susceptible to early and rapid decline in their aging years. In our fast-paced world, it is easy to get wound up, stressed, and out of sorts. But we can shift our thoughts and attitudes in ways that make us feel better. The reality we see is filtered through our thoughts and feelings.

Exercise: Breathing Your Way to Calmness

This exercise is about getting centered and promoting positive thoughts and feelings. To illustrate the point, try this simple deep-breathing exercise (modified and abbreviated from one created by well-known Buddhist monk Thich Nhat Hanh):

As you breathe in, think about calm entering your body;

As you breathe out, smile (actually physically form a smile);

As you breathe in a second time, feel yourself in the present moment;

As you breathe out again, visualize the present moment as a perfect moment.

Repeat the sequence a few times to get the full benefit of the exercise.

Activities like this brief breathing exercise take no more than a few minutes, yet they can significantly shift our thoughts and feelings in positive ways. Feeling calm, smiling, and being in the present and perfect moment can all combine to increase our sense of wellness. If this can happen for the moment, think about what experimenting with being more positive every day can do for the overall quality of our lives. We can do much to improve our lives by choosing to develop positive attitudes.

> *There is only one world, the world pressing against you at this minute. There is only one minute in which you are alive, this minute—here and now.*
> —Storm Jameson

Mike M. Milstein

STRATEGIES TO DEVELOP LIFE-GUIDING SKILLS

How can we develop the skills that are required at this life stage? For starters, we need to assess what skills we need. Some of them are already part of our response system, but we may need to modify them to fit our current situation. Others may not yet be part of our repertoire. Each of us needs to inventory our own skill strengths and weaknesses in order to decide which to concentrate on and what we have to do to learn more about them.

What motivates people to learn life skills that are necessary to navigate their aging years? The rest of the chapter focuses on life-guiding skills and the strategies that can help us acquire them as we try to create and sustain a high quality of life during our older years. You are encouraged to examine your own status regarding each of the strategies discussed below, sort through and prioritize those that are most in need of your attention, and develop plans to become more effective in applying them.

Positive Attitudes

Everything we do, feel, think, and experience flows from our attitudes. It's simple: Those who see the glass as half-empty feel and behave very differently than those of us who see the glass as half-full. The good news is that we can shift our attitudes in positive directions if we choose to do so. In fact, even if you

> *Grow old with me. The best is yet to be.*
> —Robert Browning

don't feel positive, fake it until you make it! With time, you may truly begin to feel more positive. A good starting place might be to relax and center yourself so you can promote positive feelings within yourself.

Many psychologists are beginning to practice what is referred to as positive psychology, which emphasizes potentials and strengths rather than the more traditional therapeutic focus on deficits and weaknesses (Seligman 2002). This reorientation parallels the basic beliefs that underlie resiliency: The more we emphasize the positive and the possible, the more we can experience well-being and lead quality lives.

An example of the power of

> *Hope is a risk that must be run.*
> —George Barnanas

Resilient Aging

positive thinking is the placebo effect. When medical researchers try to establish the value of an experimental drug, they often give a placebo—usually a simple sugar pill—to some of those who volunteer to try the drug in order to establish the validity of their results. However, the results quite often show that many of those who are given the placebo have the same positive outcomes as those who get the drug. Why? Those who take the placebo and respond positively are affected by the belief that they have being given the drug. Believing that they are getting a treatment that can improve their health appears to be sufficient for their bodies to respond positively. Attitudes do matter!

Being positive is part of the story. Being realistic is also important. Our aging experience is shaped by how we think about our bodies and our minds, but we need to be flexible and not be in denial about our aging. Being realistic means assessing what we need to do to function well and then moving on to engage our energies positively and creatively.

Managing Transitions

Moving into our older years means experiencing some major transitions: from worker to retiree, from offspring at home to empty nester, from health to coping with physical challenges, and, too often, from being at the center of work and family dynamics to being shunted aside. Transitioning from our middle years to later life, most of us learn that it is not simply about continuing to be who we were and do what we did. In our older years, we change and experience problems, challenges, and opportunities that were not part of our earlier lives.

> *People can't live with change if there's not a changeless core inside them. The key to the ability to change is a changeless sense of who you are, what you are about and what you value.*
> —Stephen R. Covey

To make this transition effectively, we need to look forward as well as backward. For many of us, there may be as much as a third of our lives left to experience after we retire. These additional years, our third age, are going to be different from the years that have come before. To manage them well, we need perspective and new and different life-guiding skills than those that guided us through our earlier years.

Gender Issues

Some of these skill development needs are gender specific. Sometime during our middle ages, many people begin to experience "gender crossover" (Moody, 1997), a time when we begin to explore aspects of ourselves that have been ascribed to the other gender and that we may not have developed very well. For many males, especially those who held high-status leadership positions during their middle years, there is a need to develop what is erroneously referred to as feminine attributes, such as being able to express feelings and emotions and having good listening and empathy capabilities. In contrast, many females, especially those in the present generation of older women who played nurturing and supporting roles earlier in life, may need to learn assertiveness skills, which are often erroneously seen as male attributes. In other words, both genders need to develop and express life-guiding skills that have traditionally been attributed to the other gender if they expect to live balanced and healthy lives during their older years.

Responding to Change

Before we can respond positively to the many inevitable transitions that confront us, we have to be willing to change. The barriers that cause us to resist change include the following:

> *Since old age is sure to bring us many surprises, we should learn to be more flexible in our behavior, rather than more rigid.*
> —Ram Dass

1) ***Change means loss and destabilization.*** For example, to change, we have to let go of beliefs and behaviors. As we do, our tried-and-true ways may have to give way to new-and-untried ways.
2) ***Change is confusing.*** When we begin to change, we leave the known for the unknown. We have many questions that can't be answered until we actually experience the change.
3) ***Change can disrupt established relationships***, including those that are intergenerational, spousal, with friends, and even those

with ourselves. This is a powerful barrier, regardless of what the particular change is that we are confronting.

To overcome our resistance, we need to get out of our comfort zones and develop behaviors that enable us to cope more effectively with change and transitions. For example, we need to:

- Shift our perspectives away from maintenance and toward growth;
- Develop a clear vision of what we want for ourselves now and in the future, and proactively work to make our vision become a reality;
- Realize that some of our efforts may not get us where we want to go, but rather than see them as "failures," we need to view them as learning experiences or building blocks to the development of more effective management of our transitions;
- Recognize that we will have a secure base of continuity because our basic sense of self will remain in place. Not all things will change. In fact, many things will stay the same; and
- Realize that we have accumulated experiences, wisdom, and skills over our lifetimes, which we can call upon to help us move through our transitions.

Seeking Life's Meaning

Life in our aging years is more than an extension of our middle years. We may have relatively stable personalities and behave in ways that are similar to the ways we did earlier in life, but our priorities and activities will probably change. As we age, many of us find ourselves giving more thought to the meaning of life. Why are we here? What are we supposed to do to fulfill the reasons we are here? If we choose to respond to such questions, we soon realize that we will never completely discover satisfactory answers, but that should not deter us from taking the journey.

> *The length of your life is less important than its depth.*
> —Marilyn vos Savant

Viktor Frankl (1959) believes that he and others who survived the concentration camps of World War II would have found it extremely difficult to remain alive without focusing on meaning. His experiences led him to conclude (p.162) that "a human being is not one in pursuit of happiness but rather in search of a reason to become happy … through actualizing the potential meaning inherent and dormant in a given situation." Thankfully, most of us will never have to experience such extreme negative conditions as Frankl encountered in the concentration camps, but we are still likely to find ourselves engaged with questions about the meaning of life as we age. Without meaning, it is difficult to imagine maintaining a motivated and high-quality life.

Ultimately, each of us must create and shape the meaning of our own lives. Living a meaningful life requires developing a rhythm that moves back and forth between action and reflection. Actions and outcomes can be reflected upon. Reflection can be used to improve performance in subsequent actions. Over time, as this action-reflection-action cycle is repeated, we learn, grow and develop, become more resilient, and shape the meaning of our lives.

> *It is not by muscle, speed, or physical dexterity that great things are achieved, but by reflection, force of character, and judgment; in these qualities old age is usually not only not poorer but is even richer.*
>
> —Cicero

Becoming comfortable and adept at the action-reflection-action cycle is not easy in a society in which action is viewed as taking charge and positive, while reflection is seen as passive and negative. The reality is that reflection is active, but it is not easy to see it as such because it is an internal process. We need to understand and appreciate the importance of reflection and find ways to promote it. This includes creating quiet times to be by ourselves so we can get in touch with our thoughts and feelings, recording our reflections in diaries and journals, sharing experiences and observations with friends, and learning from others who are adept at practicing the action/reflection rhythm cycle.

Reflecting about our life histories is also a good way of getting in touch with the meaning of our lives. Recalling, writing, and telling our stories can help us reconstruct the major threads of our lives and give us insights about who we have become

> *We did not change as we grew older; we just became more clearly ourselves.*
>
> —Lynn Hall

and where we may be going. This process, which is often referred to as life review, can take different forms: including autobiographical writing, creating audiotapes and videotapes, storytelling, or putting an album of photos together. Whatever form we choose, the intent is to synthesize what we have experienced, providing focus to our present lives and direction for the future. Life review also helps us realize that we have survived many personal challenges, including physical difficulties, loss of loved ones, and economic upheavals, to make it to this life stage. Awareness of our ability to respond effectively to such challenges helps us be confident that we have the resiliency required to cope with today's and tomorrow's challenges.

Pursuing Growth and Development

It is a difficult task to take charge of our aging years in a society that prefers to have its elders step aside and be passive. But those who realize the importance of taking charge of their lives are not likely to comply with these expectations. Rather, they will put their energies into gaining confidence, feeling empowered, and growing and developing. Alfred Hitchcock, James Michener, Golda Meir, Grandma Moses, Pablo Picasso, and Mother Teresa are examples of well-known older achievers who chose to take the growth and development route.

> *There are people whose watch stops at a certain hour and who remain permanently at that age.*
> —Sainte-Beuve

It is also interesting to note that centenarians, the longest living amongst us, tend to be adaptable, use their abilities well, live in the present, stay optimistic, and maintain a sense of humor (Perls and Silver).

To grow and develop, we need to take risks, make mistakes, learn from them, and taking responsibility for our lives. We are more likely to do these things in our older years if we also practiced them earlier in life, but even those who haven't can still learn to do so later in life. The process is straightforward: recognize the need, act on it, get support from others, and build on successes.

Volunteering, Engaging in Leisure Activities, and Pursuing Hobbies

Many of those who die soon after retirement do so because of a powerful sense of loss: loss of self-identity, of involvement and commitment, of an agenda to accomplish. In contrast, those who help others and develop interests earlier in life and continue to pursue them later in life tend to make the transition into their aging years more effectively. They have reasons to persist and ideas about where to put their creative energies.

It's never too early (or too late) to search out and discover challenging leisure activities and hobbies that are motivating, or to become enthused about volunteering to help others. The choices are many, but if they are going to be meaningful, we need to capitalize on our life's passions. We may decide to apply our skills and knowledge in ways that can be of help to others; concentrate on hobbies and leisure activities; or promote new avenues of growth and development through travel, reading, attending presentations, or taking courses. In fact, the search is as important as the outcomes because, in the process, we learn how to connect with others and how to find and use information that can enrich our lives.

> *If you love life, life will love you back.*
> —A. Rubenstein

Taking Care of Ourselves

If we think about our bodies as our temples, then our minds are our temples' keepers. We are probably never as aware of the truth of this statement as we are when we move into our older years. Many of us take our bodies and our minds for granted earlier in life, but now we become acutely aware of their importance. To live with resilience, we need to take care of ourselves, devoting time and effort to maintain our physical health and our mental acuity. How we do

> *If I had known I was going to live this long I would have taken better care of myself.*
> —Jimmy Durante

> *Exercise. Exercise. Exercise. It remains the single most potent anti-aging medication known to humankind.*
> —Gail Sheehy

this will vary, depending upon our age, life situation, attitudes, gender, genes, and fiscal resources. However, regardless of how we choose to do so, it is critical that we consciously work at staying physically and mentally fit. Possible strategies include:

- aerobic exercise routines that promote good muscle tone
- recreational activities that help keep us fit while involving us in activities that connect us with others
- dietary habits that keep us in a good weight range and help us ward off disease
- effective management of chronic physical problems that may not be curable, but also are not life threatening
- elimination of poor health habits such as smoking and excessive drinking
- challenging learning experiences, including such activities as reading, writing, traveling, and taking credit and noncredit courses
- housing arrangements that promote positive interactions and intergenerational contacts

Engaging in these activities will not lead to the fountain of youth, which is the message of those who suggest that "anti-aging" or even stopping aging is realistic (Chopra, 2001), but they can help us function more effectively until we near the end of our lives. Biological processes proceed regardless of our wishes, but while we can't reverse them, we can do much to slow them down. In fact, the difference between a rapid slide downward as we age versus a high-quality life experience until we approach the end of our lives is highly dependent upon the development of good physical and mental habits. Developing these habits can make the difference between functioning well and possibly extending our lifespan, or experiencing disease, decline, and a shorter life. We can improve the quality of our aging years if we moderate such inappropriate behaviors as smoking or

> *Mental activity increases throughout adult life—if the mind is kept active, interested, and useful. It will decrease by inactivity, not by aging.*
> —Hardin B. Jones

drinking and practice behaviors that emphasize good physical and mental functioning.

Decline may be a reality, but by exercising our bodies and minds we can grow, develop, and stay healthier longer. Even those who never exercised before older age can still improve their physical and mental abilities during this life stage. In fact, more than half of the people in the MacArthur Foundation's studies were able to maintain the rate of functioning they had when they became involved in the study, and a quarter of those who participated actually improved their functioning (Rowe and Kahn, 1999).

The same positive outcomes can be experienced regarding our ability to retain and extend our mental functioning. There is growing evidence that we do not have to lose our mental capabilities as we age, but to maintain mental sharpness we need to exercise our brains, just like we need to exercise our bodies. Most intelligence measures favor younger people over older people because they put an emphasis on speed of response. However, if we define intelligence as the capacity to reason, retain, and apply knowledge effectively, aging people can do just as well and, in some ways, better than younger people.

> *Minds, like bodies, will often fall into a pimpled, ill-conditioned state from mere excess of comfort.*
> —Charles Dickens

Most aging people accumulate life experiences and knowledge. To capitalize on this advantage we need to stimulate our mental capacities regularly. The means of doing so include such things as reading books and magazines; creating and participating in projects that challenge us mentally; discussing important ideas and issues; getting involved in politics; attending stimulating lectures and workshops; and taking formal classes. The more challenging and diverse our choices, the more likely we will maintain and possibly strengthen our mental capabilities.

Managing Stress

The challenges associated with aging can be quite distressful. If we don't respond to them effectively, we

> *A person without a sense of humor is like a wagon without springs—jolted by every pebble in the road.*
> —Henry Ward Beecher

are likely to experience some negative manifestations. These might be physical, such as headaches, digestive problems, inability to sleep well, or possibly even more severe responses, such as ulcers or cancer. They also can manifest as emotional distress or depression. For example, we may find ourselves unable to perform important activities, such as driving safely or remembering important information.

When negative physical and emotional distress manifestations occur, we need to focus on them, but we also need to focus on the root cause, which is stress buildup. We need to learn to manage stress more effectively so that we can make it work for us rather than against us.

Stress is simply part of life. It's what we do about it that makes the difference in the quality of our lives. This means watching for early signs of stress and developing effective responses before things become too distressful. Each of us needs to develop our own unique responses, but healthy practices such as the following can make a positive difference in how we cope with stress:

- a healthy diet, regular mealtimes, and minimal snacking between meals
- weight control
- regular exercise
- reflective practices such as meditation, tai chi, and yoga, all of which quiet the mind and body
- minimization of negative habits, such as smoking and drinking
- avoidance of situations that we find distressful
- connecting with others for mutual support

Being Open to Experimentation and Creativity

To live fully and well at any stage of life, we need to focus on growth and development, which are affected by our willingness and ability to experiment and be creative. When we experiment with different behaviors and learn effective responses, we gain confidence and become more positive about our ability to respond to life's challenges. Strength builds on strength.

As we become more creative about

> *All that is good in man lies in youthful feeling and mature thought.*
> —Joubert

relationships, play, reflection, and work, we also stimulate our brains. Good brain functioning, in turn, increases the likelihood that we will continue to lead high-quality lives. In other words, people who experiment, grow, and develop as they age stand a good chance of retaining physical health and mental alertness.

> *Do not grow old, no matter how long you live. Never cease to stand like curious children before the great mystery into which we are born.*
> —Albert Einstein

Being creative about the way we shape our older years can make an important positive contribution to the quality of our lives. Cohen (2001, p. 11) says creativity "strengthens our morale in later life; contributes to physical health as we age; enriches relationships; and is our greatest legacy." When we live creatively, we also defy society's myths about decline and dementia and act as positive role models for those who follow us into the aging years.

If we expect to exercise our creative urges, we need to get out of our comfort zones. It may be tempting to relax and coast, but the reality is that we are novices about aging, so we need to experiment with behaviors that may be more effective in our new situations. We need to reach out, make new connections, explore different activities, and let go of old habits that may no longer be appropriate or

> *Experience is the name we give our mistakes.*
> —Oscar Wilde

effective. Not all our risk-taking efforts will lead to positive results, but if they fall short, it does not mean that we have failed. Each time we leave our comfort zones, we get needed practice at being assertive. A good way to build our confidence is to start with relatively low-level risks and work up to those that are more challenging.

Reaching Out for Support and Intergenerational Connections

We are responsible for our own lives, but the support of others enhances our ability to do what needs to be done to live effectively. Of course, we also need to reciprocate if we expect others to be there for us. There are many ways of engaging in mutual support, including showing concern, assisting with physical and emotional challenges, sharing information and interests, and providing care and affection.

When we have good support, we don't tend to think about it. However, if support is not available when we need it, we become acutely aware of its absence. While we are doing well, we need to develop support systems purposefully and consciously because that's when we are most capable of attracting others to connect with us. If we have not done so, we could be in big trouble because it is not likely that others will be enthusiastic about signing on as supporters when our needs are extensive.

One of our most important supports is the intergenerational relationships we maintain with younger people, including our adult children and grandchildren, as well as with others who are older. Regular interactions with younger people help us stay in touch with emerging trends and learn what's going on and how we can be involved if we choose to do so. Regular interactions with those older than ourselves, whether they are positive or negative role models, give us important information to guide us through unknown passages as we make decisions about our own life choices. In short, intergenerational connectivity can help us become more aware of our place in life's flow, sharpen our sense about what has already transpired, better understand our current life situation, and be positive and prepared for what is yet to come.

> *I enjoy talking with very old people. They have gone before us ... and I think we do well to learn from them what it is like, easy or difficult, rough or smooth.*
> —Socrates

We are more likely to experience intergenerational connectivity if we create situations that promote this possibility. For example, we can do the following:

- seek out housing situations that put us in close proximity with younger and older people
- reach out to invite others into our lives
- volunteer in our communities in ways that promote contact, with those who are both younger and older—e.g., helping out in preschools and elementary schools or volunteering in nursing homes and hospice settings

- provide guidance, support, and positive role modeling for our adult children and grandchildren

Accepting Realistic Limitations

Aging, like gravity, eventually impacts our physical vitality and places limitations on our behaviors. We can only do as much as we are able to do, which means that we will sometimes fall short of our hopes and expectations. The issue is not whether this will happen, but how we choose to respond when it does. Seeing it as unacceptable or as failure is a sure path to depression and decline. Seeing it as a normal part of life and learning how to respond to our limited capabilities can help us move on.

> *It is human to go through negative experiences, disappointments and frustrations. It is one of the ways leading us to maturity.*
> —Fritz Kunkel and Roy E. Dickerson

It's also helpful to maintain a sense of humor, to learn to laugh about our trials and tribulations. Life is an adventure that is not always predictable or controllable. Being playful about life, even when it seems to come at us too fast or too intensely, can help us live healthy and resilient lives.

> *Humor is the balance wheel of life.*
> —Ruth Bell Graham

Those who manage to maintain positive lives as they age are realistic about limitations and learn to live comfortably with them. These are people who have figured out a pace and rhythm of life that works for them, and they don't fixate on or become embarrassed about their "shortcomings." Even centenarians who are clear about their limitations and capabilities and apply this knowledge to how they conduct their lives have shown that they can remain engaged and continue to grow.

> *Life is ten percent what you make it and ninety percent how you take it.*
> —Irving Berlin

> ### Exercise: You and Life-Guiding Skills
>
> This activity is intended to help you inventory the status of your current life-guiding skills.
> 1. Review the life-guiding skills discussed in Chapter 5. Which do you currently practice most effectively?
>   A.
>   B.
>   C.
>   D.
> 2. Which life-guiding skills do you think you need to learn more about so you can practice them more effectively?
>   A.
>   B.
>   C.
>   D.
>   E.
> 3. What do you think you need to do to improve your abilities regarding the life-guiding skills listed in number 2?
> 4. What can you do to help others who might need to improve their life-guiding skills?

In Closing

Chapter 5 began with a discussion about Bill's life-guiding skills challenges. He was a good problem solver and decision maker during the years he spent as an organizational leader prior to his retirement. But that was then. His organizational role and the status ascribed to it are no longer relevant. That life was over, and he was feeling uncomfortable about having to start all over again. Nor was he prepared for his sense of loss or clear about how to relate to others in nonauthoritarian ways. Like many of us, he hadn't reflected much about life after retirement, let alone thought about how he could apply his significant skills to his post-retirement life.

From his days as an organizational leader, Bill knew that it wasn't okay to give in when things looked bleak. He also knew that the first step to improving things was to seek out information that could clarify what was going on, so he decided to read up on aging and search the Web to learn more about how others have responded to its challenges. These activities helped him clarify the nature of the problems he was dealing with. It also gave him comfort to know that his concerns were not unique.

He thought about the years that he might still have to live and decided that he wanted to do whatever he could to make them good years. He concluded that he wasn't really starting over. He knew he would have to let go of the past and embrace his changing situation. However, he realized that many of the skills he had accumulated in his role as an organizational leader could, with some modifications, serve him well now and in the future. He also knew he would have to learn new skills to help him navigate his aging years, but based on his life experiences, he had the confidence that he could do that.

He began to keep notes, capturing his thoughts and feelings, because he wanted to be clear about how he should respond to the questions that were coming up for him. Several things emerged from his reflections. First, he concluded that he still had a lot to offer as a leader, but he realized that he would need to rechannel his interests and abilities. He started making connections with others engaged in community initiatives and soon became involved as an organizer and facilitator of service projects, sharing his skills and experiences. Second, he decided to mentor younger people who were at the beginning of their management careers and could benefit from his knowledge and insights about leadership. He called the local chamber of commerce, which put him in touch with talented young people who wanted to be mentored as they prepared for leadership roles in their organizations. Third, he realized that he needed more regularity and predictability in his life, so he began to experiment with routines that could help provide a basic structure for daily living—e.g., waking and retiring times, regular mealtimes, visits with friends and family, exercise activities, time reserved for his own growth and development, and time set aside for his volunteer work. Finally, he decided to take advantage of his newfound free time to dust off and learn more about some of his interests, such as astronomy and American history.

He started to feel better about himself and his life in retirement. He was more confident about making it through the transition from work to retirement and gaining control of his life. The future looked good.

Chapter Six

Nurturance and Support

*So long as we love, we serve; so long as we are loved by others,
I would almost say we are indispensable.*
—Robert Louis Stevenson

Nancy felt sad and lonely. Taking stock of life, she didn't like what she saw. She and Gus, her husband, had moved from Buffalo, New York, to Boca Raton, Florida, a few years ago, in search of a warmer climate. They had kept pretty much to themselves until Gus, who was ten years older than Nancy, had a heart attack and died last year. Suddenly, the most important person in her life was gone. The rest of her support system was tenuous at best. For starters, she had lost touch with many of her Buffalo friends. She'd written cards, exchanged e-mails, and traded phone calls, but she didn't have regular contacts with those friends anymore. She really hadn't made any lasting friendships or found satisfying ways of contributing her energies and passions in her new community. To make matters worse, her two grown children, both of whom lived in other parts of the country, were busy raising their own families. She realized that she deeply missed the rich and intimate relationships she used to have with her husband and children, as well as friends in her community. She was sixty-seven years old and a stranger in a strange new land. The future looked bleak. She began to question her self-worth and wondered whether anybody cared if she lived or died.

Nancy keenly felt the disparity between her need to be nurtured and supported and her seeming inability to secure these resiliency builders. Like many of us she had taken them for granted throughout her life. She had been nurtured and supported as a youngster by her parents and siblings, in the love she had experienced with her husband, as mother of her own children, with the many friends she had made over time, and as a longtime participant and volunteer in her western New York community.

Nancy gave at least as much support as she received from family and friends over the years. Much of the loss she was now feeling had to do with her inability to find adequate outlets for the considerable energies that she wanted to bring to nurturing others. Her parents and her loving husband had died; the physical distance between herself and her children, grandchildren, and friends made it difficult to find ways to support them; and lack of experience in her new community was making it quite difficult for her to figure out how to participate as a volunteer.

> *Life is made up of ever so many partings welded together.*
> —Charles Dickens

As she assessed her situation, it looked bleak and would probably get worse with time. Through death and distance she had lost many of the people who mattered to her—people who nurtured and supported her and who she, in turn, nurtured and supported. She knew it would take a lot of effort to reestablish her support network and replace the relationships she had lost with new people. However, she had little sense of how to go about meeting others even if she could gather the strength to do so.

Unfortunately, Nancy's story is not unique. Many aging people find themselves in similar circumstances. It is difficult to feel positive, let alone resilient, when those who matter are gone or no longer available to us.

The good news is that we can do much to reduce the impact of such losses by creating other nurturing and supporting relationships. Chapter Six explores the importance of nurturance and support as we age. It also examines why it is so difficult for many older people to find the nurturance and support they need and want to give to others. Finally, it describes strategies that can be used to overcome the formidable barriers to getting and giving nurturance and support in our older years.

THE IMPORTANCE OF NURTURANCE AND SUPPORT

Being nurtured and supported lets us know that we matter to others. When spouses, relatives, friends, care givers, and others support us, our well-being and our sense of self-worth are enhanced. In turn, contributing to the nurturance and support of those we care about reminds us that we can be of value to their well-being. Mutual support helps promote balanced, equitable, and caring relationships.

We need the support of others, from womb to tomb. Even the most independent and reclusive among us need to develop and maintain nurturing and supporting relationships that are deeper than

> *There is a destiny that makes us brothers. None goes his way alone. All that we send into the lives of others comes back into our own.*
> —Edwin Markham

superficial contacts. How we go about this will differ, depending on our personalities, our preferences for relating or solitude, and our time of life, but we all have an inborn need for supportive contacts with others. In fact, we are likely to suffer, physically or mentally, if we don't satisfy this need.

Connecting at a deeper level of care and support requires that we drop protective barriers and take the risk to listen fully, speak clearly and honestly, and share from the heart. This kind of intimacy can only be experienced if we set our defenses aside, become real, and focus on what is truly important. When we do so it makes it easier to find the support that can be shared between ourselves and others.

In *High Tide in Tucson*, Barbara Kingsolver ruminated about her relationship with her mate (1995, p. 270): "My dear mate and I will get to watch each other creak into old age and fall into uneasy truces with our own limbs—that's the *best* case, presuming we cleave together as we've hoped and promised." She went on to say why she was willing to participate in such a relationship: "Here today, gone tomorrow. It's the best reason I can think of to throw open the blinds and risk belief. Right now, this minute, time to move out into the grief and glory. High tide."

As Kingsolver sees it, engaging in supporting and nurturing relationships is 'high risk intimacy' in action and well worth the risks that may be required. Romantics will resonate positively with her observations and priorities. Those who are skeptical, or simply hesitant, need to know that a growing body of evidence tells us we can improve the

> *Age does not protect you from love. But love, to some extent, protects you from age.*
> —Jeanne Moreau

potential to live lives marked by well-being if we participate in meaningful relationships. For example, a study in New England found that centenarians who maintain meaningful relationships with others have better health and higher morale (Perls and Silver, 1999). Similarly, the MacArthur Foundation's studies on aging provide evidence of the connection between maintaining caring relationships with friends and relatives and exhibiting good physical and mental abilities (Rowe and Kahn, 1999).

> *Never lose sight of the fact that old age needs so little but needs that little so much.*
> — Margaret Willour

Resilient Aging

Exercise: Do You Matter to Others?

Who nurtures and supports you? Who do you nurture and support? The more conscious we are about the people who we believe are part of our support group, and why we include them in this group, the more aware we will be about their importance to our well-being. Keep this in mind as you respond to the following questions:

1. List five family members who you think are important members of your support group. What do these individuals do that makes you feel as if they support and nurture you? What do you do to nurture and support them?

Individuals	*What They Do*	*What I Do*
A.		
B.		
C.		
D.		
E.		

2. Do the same for five friends who you think are important members of your support system.

Individuals	*What They Do*	*What I Do*
A.		
B.		
C.		
D.		
E.		

3. Was it difficult for you to identify family members and friends who provide important support for you? If so, why?

4. Do you need to think more about what you do for them?

5. As you look at your lists, is your support system sufficient or do you need to expand it?

Mike M. Milstein

The Costs of Isolation

As we age, the potential for experiencing isolation increases. We are likely to lose established caring relationships through distance and death, and we may find it difficult to find the energy to develop new relationships.

Isolation is a powerful risk factor that can lead to poor health and premature death. Those who don't experience much human affection and support are likely to deteriorate and die at a faster rate than others. In fact, people who are relatively isolated have, on average, two and a half times the mortality rate of those with strong social bonds (Anderson, 1979).

About 20 percent of Americans live alone, but the percentage is much higher for people who are over sixty-five (Friedan, 1993). However, living alone does not have to equate to being lonely or isolated. For those who enjoy solitude, but are also comfortable about reaching out to connect with others, living alone may be just fine, but those who do not have the skills or motivation to reach out may risk becoming isolated.

The potential for us to be isolated is exacerbated by the fact that more people than ever before are living longer lives. In other words, there are more of us seeking nurturance and support at a time in life when it is most difficult to fulfill this need. With so many older people feeling isolated, it should not be surprising that the sixty-five-plus group, which represents about 13 percent of the general population, accounts for 25 percent of all suicides. It should also be noted that a disproportionate number of these older population suicides are by men.

> *Science has salvaged scrap metal and even found vitamins and valuable oils in refuse, but old people are extravagantly wasted.*
>
> —Anzia Yezierska

Isolation is a reality for many of those whose social relationships are severely constrained by being institutionalized. Their isolation and lack of sufficient nurturance and support contribute heavily to the fact that 25 percent of those who enter nursing homes die within a month of being admitted. This figure increases to 50 percent within six months of admissions (Friedan, 1993). The high mortality rate of institutionalized elders is due in part to their fragility and advanced age, but it is also associated with their loss of regular contacts with family and friends and the experience of living in a depersonalizing environment, which prevails in many nursing homes.

THE CHALLENGE OF ESTABLISHING NURTURING AND SUPPORTING RELATIONSHIPS

For a number of reasons, it can be difficult for older people to develop and maintain nurturing and supporting relationships. First and foremost are the attitudes about aging people, many of which we explored in chapter 1. In the 1700s, the few people who lived long enough to reach their older years were honored, respected, and even sometimes feared because they controlled so many of society's resources. Over time, these positive attitudes were replaced by an emphasis on the virtues of youth and a devaluation of older people. The stereotypical image is that the young are passionate, while the old are beyond caring. Why put resources into supporting and nurturing older people if they aren't interested in living anymore?

> *Do not let others impose upon you the mythology of "old age" ... The later years can be the happiest of one's life.*
> —Ashley Montagu

Overcoming this attitude is difficult. Those who are in the best position to provide support for older people are their own adult children. However, as much as they may empathize, these midlife offspring have had firsthand experience with the challenges of being young but not with aging. They can relate to youthful passions and needs, but they haven't had the relevant aging experience that can help them fully understand the support and nurturance needs of their parents.

Second, few of us have firsthand experience living in intergenerational family situations. This increases the likelihood of isolation for our older citizens. In the United States, only one family out of four houses and cares for its own elders. In Asian countries, about 75 percent of the elderly live in intergenerational situations (Pipher, 1999). When older people are removed from daily contact with their adult children and their grandchildren, opportunities to give and receive nurturance and support are significantly reduced.

Third, the stream of negative messages older people receive from a society that puts a premium on youth

> *Kind words can be short and easy to speak, but their echoes are truly endless.*
> —Mother Teresaa

can lead to a reduced sense of self. Older people are likely to have daily encounters that are replete with demeaning and devaluing messages. For example, when they shop, deal with bureaucrats, drive, or go for a walk, they are likely to get implicit or even explicit derogatory messages such as "Hey there, Gramps/Grandma," "Get out of the way," "Learn to drive or get off the road," or "You've got the time to wait, but I don't." In fact, many older people complain that they seem to be invisible to younger people.

Such negative messages are especially difficult to ignore when, through attrition or distance, we find our positive relationships dwindling. With increasing negative feedback and less available care and support, a self-fulfilling prophecy of being unworthy can easily set in. We may not feel as if we get any respect. Worse, like Rodney Dangerfield, we may conclude that we don't deserve to get any respect!

> *Keep away from people who belittle your ambitions. Small people always do that, but the really great make you feel that you, too, can become great.*
> —Mark Twain

Fourth, men who were in key leadership roles prior to retirement often have to learn how to give and receive nurturance and support in non-structured and nonauthoritarian situations. For many of these men, rewards that mattered during their work lives focused on success and status. Once retired, they may find it challenging to reduce their dependency on these payoffs and replace them with the rewards of intimacy, caring, and support. Sheehy followed a group of Harvard business school graduates who successfully made this transition. At their thirtieth college reunion, these men mainly shared stories about their accomplishments in the business world. But at their fortieth reunion, she says (1995, 379), "having attained an average age of sixty-six, the same men had become pussycats. The big switch was from seeking satisfaction *out there*—through the success and status of their business careers—to savoring the pleasures of a return to hearth and home. At this stage, they derived their greatest satisfaction from their intimate relationships with their wives, friends, and children, to whom they now look for understanding and support."

Strategies That Promote Nurturance and Support

Given the serious obstacles that stand in the way of getting the nurturance and support we need at this life stage, it makes little sense to sit back and wait for them to come to us. We can do much to increase the extent and quality of nurturance and support in our lives. For the remainder of the chapter, we will explore some strategies that can help us do so.

Develop a Positive Self-Image

We have to like and be at peace with ourselves if we expect to attract others to be part of our support network. If we are unhappy, grumpy, dissatisfied, and unpleasant to be around, we can hardly expect to attract care and support from others. When we consistently send negative vibrations, even those who are bound to us through family ties will stay away or at least try to minimize interactions with us.

> *First of all you have to be your own best friend.*
> —Christine Grimaldi

We can start by liking ourselves and behaving with compassion and forgiveness. Some of us learn to like ourselves early in life and continue to do so throughout the rest of our lives. For others who have not had this experience, it will probably require breaking old habits and learning new ones. Most important, we have to develop the habit of practicing positive and supportive self-talk. If we focus on our strengths rather than our weaknesses, we send ourselves positive messages that promote self-worth.

> *It is not easy to find happiness in ourselves, and it is not possible to find it elsewhere.*
> —Agnes Replier

Developing a positive self-image may also require sharing our concerns, thoughts, and hopes with others. Talking with people who listen well and are nonjudgmental can clarify our reflections and help us develop a more balanced and positive sense of self. As we share reflections and feelings with people who accept us as we are, we also build confidence about being able to reach out to others.

Risk Intimacy

Intimacy based on mutual caring and support is important at all stages of life. However, the accelerating loss of those we care about as we grow older may require us to rethink and redefine the meaning of intimacy in our lives. Our parents, if not dead, may be in decline or in their final years. Our adult children may have little time to spare for us. Longtime friends may have moved elsewhere or may be coping with serious and debilitating health problems.

> *Remember, spend some time with your loved ones, because they are not going to be around forever.*
> —George Carlin

> *The best mirror is an old friend.*
> —English proverb

The longer we live, the more we experience family and friendship losses, and the more we need to find ways of creating new and different kinds of caring relationships. Friendships become all the more important to us as we age because they provide opportunities to experience respect and care. We need this support more than ever when we are going through the major life transition called aging.

How can we create new meaningful relationships? For starters, we can learn from older people who have done this successfully. Studies of centenarians show that those who function well, despite the fact that they have outlived their families and friends, are able to do so because they have the ability and desire to reach out and develop new meaningful relationships. They attract people by being positive, engaging, and supportive. They purposefully and creatively seek new relationships because they intuitively know that intimacy is vitally important to their well-being (Perls and Silver, 1999).

Sexual expression is one important form of intimacy. In chapter two, we explored the myths associated with sex, or more accurately, the supposed lack of it as we age. However, there is persuasive evidence that many older people remain active sexually. A significant majority even report that sex is better now than when they were younger. One reason for this deepening interest is that older people have

> *The age of a woman [or man] doesn't mean a thing. The best tunes are played on the oldest fiddles.*
> —Sigmund Z. Engel

little to prove by being sexual gymnasts. They are usually more interested in pleasing and having heart connections with their partners. In short, many older people who engage in sexual activities have mellowed and have come to appreciate the deeper connections, the intimacy, and the romance that can be experienced in a caring sexual relationship.

Of course, there are also many nonsexual ways to express intimacy. Our older years can be a time when we discover the joys of nonsexual caring, nurturing, and supportive relationships with others. Such intimacies are based on deep sharing rather than on sexual relations.

> *To grow old is to pass from passion to compassion.*
> —Albert Camus

To broaden our thinking, it may be helpful to think about intimacy as adventure rather than romance. Romance is associated with yearning, and it is directly linked to sex in many of our minds. Adventure, on the other hand, as defined by Webster, is "an exciting or very unusual experience." Exciting and unusual experiences are individually defined, but however we do so, the fact is that when we are having adventures, we feel more fully alive. If we free ourselves from the narrower images of romance, we can expand our thinking about intimacy and increase the probability of experiencing it in our lives. In the process, we are also more likely to receive nurturance and support from others who share our adventures.

ENCOURAGE POSITIVE REGARD AND FEEDBACK

We are more likely to feel worthy of care, support, love, and nurturance if we give and get positive regard and feedback. We may have to expand on or even replace the sources of positive regard we counted on in the past, such as people at our former worksites and our nuclear families. Positive feedback that we got and gave without much effort at earlier life stages may now have to be fostered and purposefully built into the fabric of our lives. But we can make it happen. For example, we can:

> *A friend is one who knows all about you and likes you anyway.*
> —Christi Warner

- Practice positive feedback that supports the growth and

development of others. The more we do so, the more we are likely to get positive feedback in return;
- Provide support to others in times of need, such as when someone is in the hospital or is dealing with the death of a loved one. Similarly, we can mark special positive occasions such as birthdays and anniversaries with our friends;
- Create meaningful ceremonial events that recognize, honor, and celebrate aging people's efforts and achievements. These include honoring those who volunteer in community improvement efforts; providing for the needs of elders who require help getting around or getting their meals; or simply being positive role models for living long and positive lives. Recognizing each other is a powerful positive regard and feedback strategy;
- Create blessing and welcoming ceremonies. These are communal events that honor elders and promote friendships. They provide opportunities for people to come together to recognize and benefit from the sense of belonging to a caring and supportive community; and
- Reach out and rekindle positive regard and feedback relationships that may have dwindled over the years. We can reach out via mail, e-mail, phone, or other means to family members, old friends, and people with whom we worked. Such efforts can reconnect us with people who are important to us and remind us of the continuity between our past, our present, and our future.

Foster Interdependent Relationships

Most of us place high value on being independent. We want to be able to take care of ourselves and be comfortable about being by ourselves. But we are also social beings who benefit from meaningful relationships with others. Interdependent people function well on their own, but they also realize that they can also benefit greatly when they connect positively and meaningfully with others.

Healthy interdependent relationships are marked by giving and receiving support, helping all involved maintain well-balanced quality lives. Interdependent people know that cooperating and sharing is important, and they seek out others who feel the same way. Over time, like-minded people form all sorts of support groups, which are just as important in our older years as they are in our earlier years.

Many older people have difficulty establishing and maintaining meaningful support groups. In reality, there are probably more possibilities available to us than we are aware of, but we do have to be assertive about seeking meaningful relationships, especially those that foster a healthy balance between giving and receiving, both of which are important. As we

> *It is one of the beautiful compensations of life that no man can sincerely try to help another without helping himself.*
> —Ralph Waldo Emerson

age, some of us encounter physical or mental challenges that require the support of others. Others may still function, but they will also receive benefits from their participation and support because doing something meaningful for others makes us feel good about ourselves.

What are our most likely sources of supportive relationships? Each of us has our own unique needs, interests, and abilities, so we may place different priorities on the kinds of relationships that are important to us. However, regardless of our individual preferences, there are certain kinds of interdependent relationships that most of us need:

- **Intimate connections.** Preferably, this involves connecting with a caring person with whom we have developed a shared life over time, someone who knows us better than

    > *Old ladies [and men] take as much pleasure in love as do the young ones.*
    > —Abbe' de Brantome

    anyone else. Of course, such long-term situations may not be desired by or available to everyone, but even in such situations, there are alternative loving relationships that can be developed. Whatever form it takes, shared intimacy provides a unique form of support and nurturance that is difficult to match.
- **Intergenerational family connections.** These include connections with siblings, adult children, grandchildren, and extended family members. These relationships keep us in touch with our histories, provide outlets for our desire to give to those we care about, and can be a primary source of support for

present and future life needs. Ironically, many of us spend the first half of our lives putting distance between ourselves and our families as we establish independent adult lives and create our own families. Then we spend the second half of our lives reaching out to reconnect with our family.

- *Friendships*. Friends are people who freely choose to support each other. The longer friendships persist, the closer they tend to become, and the more we recognize their value. The good news is that we have more time to nurture these friendships as we age.

Replace Lost Relationships

We can't assume that longtime supporters will remain available as we age. Distance, disability, and death all chip away at our established relationships. Our children grow up, take on adult responsibilities, and may move away to pursue careers, making it difficult for them to be mainstays in our lives. Similarly, once we retire, we lose connections with work mates we've left behind, most of whom are still busy and are not likely to put a priority on socializing with us. Our friends may move away, become infirm, or die. Or we may be the ones who move, leaving our homes when maintenance seems too difficult or the space feels too large once we are empty nesters—or we simply depart for warmer climates.

When we lose caring relationships, our world seems to shrink. We need to replace these losses or else we stand a good chance of becoming increasingly isolated. We need to reach out, take risks, and initiate new relationships with others who we think will be able to share our interests. This may be easier for the young-old than the old-old, and for the extroverts more than introverts. Regardless, we need to focus on revitalizing our support networks.

> *A friend is a gift you give yourself.*
> —Robert Louis Stevenson

Develop Non-People Alternatives

The more we broaden our sources of support, the better. There are many ways to compensate for the lack of supportive relationships with people or to enrich our lives even if we are fortunate enough to have such relationships. For example, pets are readily available to give and receive love and care, so they can be extremely important to older people. Pets can have the kind of healing effects that we hope for in supportive relationships, including lowered blood pressure and cholesterol levels, reduced psychiatric disturbances, and reduced stress. In fact, older people who have pets may be more likely to live longer than those who do not (Pipher, 1999).

Other non-people choices can promote support. Gardening takes on greater significance for those who enjoy planting, maintaining, and harvesting flowers, vegetables, or fruit gardens. Others may take pleasure from listening to or creating music, expressing artistic interests through, for example, photography or painting, or exploring the thinking of creative people through reading. What works for one person may not work for another. Each of us needs to discover outlets for our passions that are motivating, keep us connected with our surroundings, and contribute to our sense of being nurtured and supported.

Select Caregivers Carefully

As we age, we may need to receive some form of care from others. Some of our caregivers may be volunteers drawn to us through family or friendship ties. We may seek others like doctors, geriatric specialists, nursing home staff, counselors, and others who are professionals, or our families may enlist as caregivers if we are not able to do things for ourselves. As we grow older, we may spend increasing amounts of time with both kinds of caregivers, so it is important that we maintain relations with them that are supporting and nurturing.

Family members or friends will provide support willingly if they value us or they will do so grudgingly and resent the efforts required if they feel negative about us. There is growing evidence that many of the friends and family members who willingly give care to older people find that they get as much from the relationship as they give to it. For example, one study shows that caregivers report gaining a stronger feeling of purpose in their lives and having improved physical health as a result of providing care (Moody, 1997). Another study shows that fully 50 percent of the daughters who provide care for their mothers feel that this activity has enriched their mother-daughter relationship, while only 5 percent feel that it has had a negative impact on the relationships (Friedan, 1993).

These findings point to the reciprocal nature of nurturance and support between caregivers and those who receive their care. This is a reassuring finding, given the growing care giving role that members of the baby boomer generation are playing with their long-living parents. The payoffs for both generations can be significant (Pipher, 1999, p. 127): "These long, hard years can work only if everyone can agree to tolerate imperfection and to stay the course. This stage in the life of a family requires the skills of both the older generation and the baby boomers ... Successful resolution of this stage allows the old-old to feel respected and at peace with their families. They learn to accept the nurturing that children offer. The young get the chance to grow up and truly be adults." It is also important to note that many boomers have to cope with challenges from their children as well as from their parents. In fact, the boomers are becoming known as the "in-between generation" because of the responsibilities to simultaneously care for their aging parents and their children, many of whom remain dependent far longer than young adults did in the past.

Professional caregivers who help sustain us as we age need to be chosen carefully for their interest and ability in providing genuine care and support, as well as for their technical skills. We need professional caregivers who really do care about us, who see us as individuals with challenges and deserving of respect and support, not as commodities to be processed. Many of us remember the family doctor as being someone who made house calls, knew us, and cared about our well-being. Getting such personalized and caring treatment today is more difficult, but if we shop around, we can still find truly caring caregivers. We don't have to settle for cold and clinical treatment.

> *If you haven't any charity in your heart, you have the worst kind of heart trouble.*
> — Bob Hope

Promote Positive and Caring Environments

Our environments—our homes, our families, our neighborhoods, the places we meet friends, and the community organizations we participate in—are all important to our well-being. If they are positive settings, they can encourage supporting and nurturing relationships.

It is difficult to sustain such environments as we age. In part, this is because of the losses we incur, including the end of relationships at work, adult children moving on to conduct their own lives, and the loss of friends through decline and death. In part, it is also due to the rapid rate of social change, which makes it less likely that churches, synagogues, neighborhoods, and families will serve as the foundation of our support as they used to. However, we can do many things to promote caring environments, including the following:

- Shape our living situations in ways that minimize isolation and promote support and nurturing. If our homes are large but we don't want to leave them, we can invite others to share them with us. Alternatively, we can pool resources with others to create other forms of caring and shared living arrangements.
- Participate in community initiatives intended to promote interdependent relationships and enrich the lives of community members. Volunteering our time and skills can help achieve environments that are more positive and give us a sense of well-being because we have made meaningful contributions.

> *It seems to me nowadays that the most important task for someone who is aging is to spread love and warmth wherever possible.*
> —Käthe Kollwitz

- Spend more time in and around natural settings, such as community parks, hiking trails, and the countryside that surrounds our communities. We can also create beautiful natural settings around our own homes by, for example, putting in flower beds or building ponds and fountains. Connecting with nature can help create a sense of belonging, balance, proportion, and meaning. Both our natural and our man-made environments can positively contribute to our well-being.
- Pressure the media to present a more balanced picture of older people in the community. This is important if we expect younger people to be positive about relating with older people in caring, supportive, and respectful ways. If more stories that are run

in the press, on TV, and on the radio are positive and caring, a healthier image concerning aging and aging people can be created in the community.

Use Political Power

Today's older population is large. Many are also better off financially than earlier generations of older people. This is due to a variety of factors, including the establishment of social security and pension plans, as well as from reaping the benefits of participating in a robust economy, at least until the recent recessionary climate. The growing size of the aging group and its significant financial clout contribute to its expanding political influence, which is being employed to impact the public's willingness to support the needs of aging people.

Political influencing initiatives clearly increase the potential of securing support and nurturance for aging people. For example, in the United States, Maggie Kuhn and the Gray Panthers led the way in the 1970s and, in the process, proved that the older population could get political leaders to respond to its unique needs. The Panthers took on hearing aid scams, pressured Congress for better health care for seniors, and lobbied for passage of the Age Discrimination Employment Act. Other groups, most notably the American Association for Retired People (AARP) have also played key influencing roles. The results of such efforts have begun to add up—providing housing for poor older adults, protecting resources devoted to the Social Security system, reforming the health system, passing regulations aimed at nursing home excesses, as well as establishing rules against age discrimination in the workplace.

It should also be noted that not all the political influencing initiatives mounted by organizations that focus on aging are aimed solely at the special interest needs of older citizens. In fact, there is growing recognition of the responsibility of the older population to give back to society for the many opportunities that it has been given.

> *Saving the world may be a matter of sowing a seed, not overturning a tyrant, that we do what we can.*
>
> —May Sarton

As evidence of this recognition, politically active older citizen organizations have been at the forefront of efforts for change and improvement that go well beyond their members' narrow needs. For

Resilient Aging

example, the Gray Panthers opposed the war in Vietnam, and the AARP partnered with the Children's Defense Fund to seek better prenatal and child health services. Such efforts give voice to the belief that wisdom, which comes with age, can and should be shared for the betterment of society.

Exercise: Nurturance, Support, and You

This activity is intended to help you clarify what you currently do and what you may need to think about doing to get the nurturance and support you want.

1. Review the nurturance and support strategies described in chapter 6. Which do you now practice most effectively?
   A.
   B.
   C.
   D.
2. Which do you think you need to do before you can practice other strategies more effectively?
   A.
   B.
   C.
   D.

In Closing

It's time to find out what Nancy has done to get the nurturance and support she needs. Nancy and Gus left their longtime home and their many friends in western New York to move to a warmer climate. When Gus died, Nancy found herself isolated. The people she cared about, her friends and her adult children, lived far away, and Gus died before they had enough time to make strong connections in her new community. She was lonely, frustrated, and felt the need to relate with others in ways that could lead to opportunities for giving and receiving nurturance and support.

After much reflection, Nancy realized that she would become more and more isolated if she didn't make the effort to find the support and nurturance she needed. Thinking about her situation, she concluded that she had lost her main supporter when Gus died, but she also realized that there were things she could do to try to fill the huge nurturance gap this left. She reached out to old friends and to her children. She phoned more frequently and let them know that she needed their support and said that she also wanted to be able to support them. As important, she took steps to develop nurturing and supporting relationships in her new setting. For example, she found ways of meeting people with similar interests by selectively attending activities at the local senior center, signing up for adult education courses at the nearby community college, learning ballroom dancing, and joining the local gardening club. She also volunteered to make fund-raising calls for the local senior center, which was seeking money to expand and diversify its space so it could attract intergenerational audiences. Along with several other highly effective volunteers, she was honored at an event that celebrated the successful opening of this new space. Finally, she adopted a dog from the local animal shelter and was delighted to find that she and her pet quickly bonded.

It was not long before she started to feel better about herself and more enthusiastic about life. She realized that she was on the way back, and that she was able to create and maintain a life marked by nurturance and support.

Chapter Seven

Purposes and Expectations

This time, like all times, is a very good one,
if we but know what to do with it.

——Ralph Waldo Emerson

John was scared and perplexed. He was two years into retirement, in good health, and had sufficient resources to support his lifestyle. He remembered how excited he was a few years before he retired, how anxious he was to have the life of leisure he anticipated, especially after so many years of being tied to a desk job in a big organization. He could hardly wait to hit the golf links and take fishing trips with his buddies without having to crowd these pleasures into the weekend hours when he wasn't mowing the lawn, shoveling snow, or taking on home improvement projects. However, like many other retirees, he soon discovered that endless golfing and fishing did not leave him feeling fulfilled. In the past, these activities provided an escape from the stresses of work and gave him the opportunity to get together with his friends for some exercise and a few laughs. But as much as he liked golfing and fishing, he was beginning to realize that they were only a part of the mosaic of life. He was growing bored with the sameness, predictability, and routines he had purposefully created in his life. Nobody had told him that his notion of a great retirement might turn into the feeling of being trapped in a meaningless life, but this seemed to be what was happening. He remembered how his father talked about hating his retirement, how he complained about having too much time on his hands and having nothing to do with it. His dad, who was in good health when he retired, died from a heart attack just four years later. John began to realize that his dad had lost his zest for living because he hadn't created new meaning. His mom, on the other hand, was still in good health and enthused about her life. She seemed to blossom after her children left home, developing new interests and friendships and becoming active as a community volunteer. John knew that he was at a junction in the road: like his mother, he needed to discover ways of establishing meaning and creating challenges in his life or he might become depressed and, like his father, die prematurely.

John had romanticized life after retirement. He had bought into the notion that retirement was about leisure, play, and relaxation, a reward for the hard work and responsibilities that marked his adult life. His image of retirement was of ease and pleasure,

> *A perpetual holiday is a good working definition of hell.*
> —George Bernard Shaw

weekends without end, a time to kick back and enjoy life. For a short while, it did indeed feel like a good life, but soon it began to feel more like a self-imposed prison with too much predictability and not enough variety, challenge or fulfillment.

Like most of us, John hadn't received much useful advice about how to prepare for the next stage of life. His employer had provided specific information, but it was mainly about being sure his departure went smoothly. It included instructions about returning his keys, clearing out his workspace, and turning in important documents. The organization even provided a little information about financial planning and benefits. However, no information was provided concerning quality-of-life issues or about establishing meaning and priorities for life after retirement.

John had not given much thought to life after retirement, beyond the expectation of doing lots of fishing and golfing. His friends were of little help either. Most of the friends who had retired had done so only recently, and they were still enthusiastic about expanded opportunities to travel, play, and relax. Those who were retired long enough to reflect about the gaps between their initial expectations and the realities they encountered were either not able or willing to verbalize their concerns.

Thus, with little guidance and a growing sense that something was wrong, John found himself scared and depressed. He had the potential to live another thirty or more years, almost as long as the years he had worked. If this potential turned out to be a reality, what was he going to do with these years?

Chapter 7 is about the relevance of meaning, purposes, and expectations in our older years. We will explore why they are so important to our well-being, the benefits they provide, the barriers that get in the way as we try to create and clarify meaning, and the strategies we can use to become more motivated and energized about our lives and our futures.

The Importance and Benefits of Purposes and Expectations

Why worry about purposes and expectations? Why not just sit back and let life slide by? Perhaps it is because the human condition leaves us having to choose between despair and growth. As Kingsolver so aptly puts it (1995, p. 16), "For every forebrain solemnly cataloging the facts of a harsh landscape, there's a rush of intuition behind it crying out: High tide! Time to move out into the glorious debris. Time to take this life for what it is."

> *To strive, to seek, to find, and not to yield.*
> —Alfred Lord Tennyson

What makes life worth living? The answers you get to this question will depend on whom you ask. However, it will probably have something to do with being challenged, growing, and believing that our lives require purpose and meaning.

We feel most alive and energized when we are challenged and motivated to achieve. Babies try to understand what is being communicated to them and make their needs and wants known to their caregivers. Children try to develop ways of belonging, especially with their peers, and seek to learn the skills needed to succeed in school. Young adults are challenged to earn a living and make a place for themselves in society. Middle-aged people focus on relationships, career development, building a resource base, and family responsibilities. Older people also are challenged, but the challenges are different from those of earlier times in life. At this stage, it is more about things like staying healthy, growing, spirituality, and leaving a legacy.

> *What adventures can we now set out on to make sure we'll be alive when we die?*
> — Anatole Broyard

> *For the unlearned old age is winter. For the learned it is the season of the harvest.*
> — Hasidic Saying

What's unique about purposes and expectations during our older years is that we no longer have extensive externally driven demands and expectations placed on us. We have navigated our way through a labyrinth of parental, spousal, offspring, friendship, community, career, and societal expectations. Our lives have been significantly shaped by these expectations, whether we bought into them or rejected them. But now we find ourselves at a stage of life where externally driven expectations are reduced to a minimum. No more parental pressures, no more work demands, and no more young children. We may still get lots of unsolicited advice about what we should and shouldn't be doing, but we don't have to listen to it.

The sense of liberation from these external demands and expectations is real, but we need to remember that they had provided us with purposes and expectations that now need replacing or our lives may become less meaningful. We need to take charge if we want to be able to transition successfully into our older years. There are persuasive reasons to focus on purposes and expectations as we age:

- Choosing to live purposefully, to grow and develop, opens us to becoming adventurers. We are finished with many of our former responsibilities, and we live in a time that is full of opportunities. For example, did you know that we can access fifteen times the knowledge that was available to Aristotle, and that we are able to travel farther in a single journey than Marco Polo did in his entire lifetime?

> *Life is too much trouble unless one can get something big out of it.*
> —Willa Cather

- Responsibilities earlier in life may have kept us from realizing our dreams and wishes. For example, we may have had to set aside our desire to learn to fly, play the piano, or create a beautiful garden. Whatever we weren't able to experience when we were younger can, potentially, be actualized during our aging years.

> *You never know how soon it will be too late.*
> —Ralph Waldo Emerson

- Being useful to others, as well as to ourselves, is more satisfying than marking time. We can benefit when we nurture others of our own generation who are not as able, and we can leave a legacy behind by nurturing the generations that follow us. Nurturing provides rewards for the giver as well as the

> *If you continually give, you will continually have.*
> —Chinese proverb

receiver: As we give, our sense of well-being is heightened, and our connections with those around us are extended. Even our immune systems are boosted when we give to others—they are positively affected when we feel in control, have a future orientation, and are purpose driven.

- Having meaningful purposes helps us feel vital and fully alive. They help us grow and develop, become more complex, and get more in touch with ourselves and our environment. The alternative, shutting down, leads to depression and alienation.

> *The greatest good fortune for the old is to have projects, to have days filled with useful and interesting work, to never be bored.*
> —Helen Nearing

- Clarifying purposes and setting expectations for achievement gets our adrenaline running and helps us cope with stress better. Setting meaningful purposes and expectations provides the foundation for the experience of excitement, enthusiasm, and feeling fully alive.

- People who are clear about purposes and are motivated to achieve them are likely to remain at a relatively high level of physical and mental functioning. This was found to be the case by the MacArthur Foundation's studies of aging Americans (Rowe and Kahn). Similar findings have been established about the physical and mental well-being of aging people who are as diverse as the Abkhasians, who live in the mountainous Black Sea area of Russia, and the Sidamo people of Ethiopia. Both the Abkhasians and the Sidamos remain active and integrated into their community's social fabric in old age, and they are viewed as useful to others (Cox, 1993).

> *People don't grow old. When they stop growing, they become old.*
> —Anonymous

- We have the opportunity to shift our attention away from worldly matters and toward exploration of spiritual matters during our older years. This is the time when we are most able to search for meaning and discover our place in the larger scheme of things. It can also be a time of reflection and wisdom building if we identify significant purposes and develop creative strategies that can engage us for years to come.

> *Not everything that can be counted counts and not everything that counts can be counted.*
> —Albert Einstein

- Finally, purposes and expectations remain relevant even as we approach our final years. Older people can be divided into two groups. The *young-old*, or those who remain healthy and maintain full lives, is mainly composed of people in their sixties and seventies, but also includes healthy people in their eighties and beyond. The *old-old*, or those who have become debilitated and whose daily lives are severely curtailed, is composed mainly of people in their eighties and beyond, but also includes those who may have become debilitated in their sixties and seventies. Those in the young-old group can lead vigorous lives, relatively unhampered by physical or mental constraints if they are guided by meaningful purposes and expectations. Even those in the old-old group have the potential to turn deficits into opportunities if they choose to let go of things they can't do physically and use their time and energy to do what they can still do, reflect about their life's experiences, and share their wisdom.

> *My seventies were interesting and fairly serene, but my eighties are passionate. I grow more intense as I age.*
> —Florida Scott-Maxwell

> *The closer we come to death, the closer we come to reality and truth.*
> —Gay Gaer Luce

- As we age, we have more freedom to craft our own purposes and expectations with minimal interference from others. But there is little precedent. The world has

> *I began to have an idea of my life ... as the gradual discovery and growth of a purpose which I did not know.*
> —Joanna Field

had little prior experience with so many people living so long. We have scant knowledge about how purposes, meaning, and expectations are shaped at this stage of life. We find ourselves in a new land, one that has been relatively unexplored by many others before us. In part, this is because most people in prior generations did not live so long, and many of those who did were not as assertive about seeking out purposes for their aging years. This is changing with the current generation of older people, and it will change even more with the baby boomers who are right behind them.

Exercise: How Do You Want to Spend Your Older Years?

There are only twenty-four hours a day, seven days a week, and twelve months a year available to each of us. Do you know how you want to spend your time? Are you clear about your priorities? Do you think they might change in the future? A good sense of your priorities can facilitate planning and allocating time in ways that help you achieve them.

This exercise can help you decide whether you are using time in ways that are important to you. Like all of us, you have only 100 percent of time at your disposal. How have you been using it? How do you want to use it now and in the future? Allocate the percentages of time according to your preferences among the categories listed below. If there are any categories listed that are not among your priorities, simply put a "0" in its place. Also feel free to add other categories that may be important to you. Do your time allocation for each of the time periods noted—*the past ten years, now, and over the next five years,* and *life beyond the next five years.*

Percent of Time Allocation by Categories

Categories	Past ten years	Over the next five years	Beyond the next five years
Health			
Paid Work			
Recreation			
Reflection/Spirituality			
Relationships			
Self-Development			
Volunteering			
Other:			

1. Was it difficult to decide about the allocations? If so, why?
2. Are there major time shifts from the past decade and the next five years? If so, what are they? Why?
3. Did you identify major shifts from the next five years to life after that time? If so, what are they? Why?
4. Is there a good match between how you want to spend your time and how you actually do spend it? If not, what can you do about it?

Life in our older years can be an amazing journey, especially as we shed responsibilities and gain the freedom to focus on the meaning of our lives. We can grow and develop as human beings and become more at peace with ourselves, but to do so we need to reduce our reliance on ego, drop our facades, confront our fears, and clarify our priorities.

Becoming focused and purposeful about life as we age is particularly important because we know that our lives are finite. Much like a pilot who is getting ready to take off and can see the end of the runway coming up, our time is limited. As we approach the end of our life's runway we become less tolerant of superficially frittering away our time. When a commodity is limited, greater value is placed on it. We feel the urgency to get on with important priorities while we still have the time to do so. Life becomes more precious.

> *The closing years of life are like the end of a masquerade party when all the masks are dropped.*
> —Arthur Schopenhauer

What Gets in Our Way?

Many barriers can constrain us as we attempt to clarify purposes and establish expectations. The environment we live in creates some barriers, while others are internal, within ourselves. The more we become aware of these barriers, the better able we will be to respond to them effectively.

> *A problem is a chance for you to do your best.*
> —Duke Ellington

Environmental Barriers

The mythologies and images about aging that prevail in our culture are, as noted, mostly negative. If we believe them, we will be left with a sense of dread about our older years because they portray aging as a time of decline, inability, and diminishing worth. These images are pervasive and confront us every day. They vary from

> *I will never be an old man. To me, old age is always fifteen years older than I am.*
> —Bernard Baruch

thoughtless comments by younger people on the streets and in the shops, to images on television and in newspapers that depict two opposite and unrealistic pictures—pitiable oldsters who are in rapid decline or vigorous oldsters who are preoccupied with holding off aging by focusing on earlier life stage challenges and activities.

These negative images also dominated the gerontology literature because they have been based on skewed information collected from institutionalized older people. However, recently, gerontologists have been collecting information that is more balanced and is leading to realistic conclusions. Unfortunately, they are finding it difficult to get their findings published (Friedan, 1993).

Perpetuation of these myths and images can hinder our ability to grow and develop in our older years. For example, consider the impact of the following images:

- **Youth is a time of vigor, so old age must be a time of decline.** Besides being erroneous, this dichotomous view distracts us from developing a more accurate picture of our aging years as a life stage with its own unique challenges and potentials. As Morrie Schwartz reminds us (Albom, 1997, p. 118), "As you grow older, you learn more. If you stayed at twenty-two, you'd always be as ignorant as you were at twenty-two. Aging is not just decay, you know. It's growth."
- **Old age is a time to rest and conserve our energy.** We are supposed to get our just rewards, rest and leisure, in return for our many years of work and responsibilities. As I have related, my own grandfather bought into this message. In his mid-sixties, he put a rocking chair on his porch and rocked the rest of his life away, until he died in his early eighties. In the process, he lost his physical stamina and his mental acuity. The point is that endless rest leads to stagnation. We need challenges and stimulation to remain vital.

> *It is better to wear out than to rust out.*
> —Richard Cumberland

The power of words on our beliefs and behaviors is great.

Resilient Aging

Unfortunately, most of the words used to describe our aging years are negative. We need to create more realistic and positive language that supports our efforts to grow, develop, and establish meaningful lives. For example, take the word "retirement," which literally means *leaving* and *desisting*. The reality is that most of us are intent on arriving and becoming as we age. Why not look at aging as a time of transition, not giving way to the end of life? As noted earlier, we might do better to refer to this life stage as *pro*tirement (Hudson, 1991), a word that is positive and active, instead of *re*tirement, a word that is negative and passive.

A related problem is that we live in a culture that prizes information over wisdom. Our society is remarkably efficient about creating and disseminating large amounts of information, most of which we need to help us manage family and work tasks. But wisdom is more than the mere collection and dissemination of information. It is the distillation of life's experiences and the creation of meaning, partly to enrich our own lives and partly to give back to others. Being older does not automatically mean being wiser, but aging people have lived long lives and do have the time to reflect about meaning, which, if they so choose, makes it possible to develop and apply wisdom. However, even if they pursue wisdom, if it is not valued, supported, and rewarded, as is often the case in our society, older people's input will not be sought or respected.

Those who are most susceptible to feeling obsolete are institutionalized older people. Unless caregivers challenge them and provide opportunities for growth and development, they are likely to stagnate. Tracy Kidder, an astute observer of human behavior, relates a dialogue (1993, p. 126) between two nursing home residents that underscores this dilemma. One says, "Everybody who comes in and goes out tells you how good you have it in here." The other responds, "I'll tell the next one, you can swap places with me anytime you want."

> *There must be more to life than just eating and getting bigger.*
> —Trina Paulus

Internal Barriers

Our perceptions affect our ability to lead meaningful lives. In fact, it could be said that our perceptions

> *Man is what he believes.*
> —Chekhov

shape our realities. Do we hold negative or positive perceptions of the world around us? Is the glass half-full or half-empty?

The good news is that while we may have to deal with challenges, we can choose how we think about them and how we respond to them. If we see ourselves as victims who are unable to cope, we will send ourselves negative messages and seek confirming negative evidence, which can lock us into an ever-tighter circle of unhappiness: "Poor me, I'm stuck and I probably always will be stuck." On the contrary, if we see ourselves as capable human beings in charge of our own lives, we will send ourselves positive messages and seek confirming positive evidence. We need to emphasize and practice positive perspectives that can move us to believe in possibilities, expectations, and growth experiences.

> *Life is full of misery, loneliness, and suffering—and it is all over much too soon.*
> — Woody Allen

One example of the power of perspectives has to do with our health. Most of us will remain healthy as we age. In fact, about 80 percent of us will lead full lives and effectively manage daily activities well into our eighties and possibly beyond our eighties. However, a minority of us will have to cope with chronic health problems, and they are likely to increase as we age, if for no other reason than the fact that our immune systems are probably not as strong as they were when we were younger.

Even when we are confronted by chronic health challenges, we don't have to despair and act like victims. We can learn to live with them. In fact, most people with chronic health problems do continue to live full lives: only about 10 percent of those sixty-five and older who have chronic problems live restricted lives (Sheehy, 1995). We can even live well with such serious health challenges as diabetes if we exercise regularly and are careful about our diets.

> *Sure, parts of me ache ... but parts of me are still having fun after all these years, too.*
> —Gene Perret

We can also change how we respond to physical challenges caused by accidents, such as taking a bad fall or being in a car crash. We don't have to behave like victims if we are confronted with accident-related health issues. Through a combination of physical therapy and acceptance, we can maintain a good quality of life following losses associated with an accident. Many people confront extreme challenges and manage to maintain meaningful lives. For example, Christopher Reeves, who, among other things, played Superman in the movies, was paralyzed in a fall from a horse. Through much effort and a positive attitude, Reeves improved enough to come back as an actor and to advocate for others suffering similar difficulties.

Another challenge for those who hope to live with purpose and expectations is to guard against excessive routines and predictability. The longer we live, the more potential there is to establish patterns of behavior that make us feel secure and comfortable, which can be positive,

> *The chains of habit are too weak to be felt until they are too strong to be broken.*
> —Samual Johnson

but if they become highly predictable and dominate our lives, over time we may live with less intensity and pay only partial attention to what is going on. Two powerful psychological forces may cause this to happen:

- **Plateauing**, a period of time when life remains calm and quiet, can be a positive and healthy period of reflection and consolidation between times of growth and development. However, it can also become a trap if we feel stuck and have little belief that we will get unstuck or that things will ever improve. If we plateau, or stay in a stuck place for very long, we slowly lose enthusiasm, and a sense of hopelessness can set in (Milstein and Henry 2008).
- **Habituation** occurs when we decrease our responses to persistent stimulation that may be bothersome to us. Blocking out unnecessary distractions, such as airplanes flying low over our homes when they are landings at a nearby airport, is a healthy response. However, we might also choose to reduce our consciousness about bothersome and repetitive stimulus sources that also enable us to experience the wonderful joys and adventures that are all around us. For instance, after

> *The fixity of a habit is generally in direct proportion to its absurdity.*
> —Proust

hiking on a trail many times, we may become habituated, oblivious to the smells, sights, and sounds that are all around us. We need to be present, be aware of our surroundings, and experience the fullness of life or our days will quickly slide by. Take the story of an older man who did all he could to avoid habituation (Pipher 1999, p. 133). He even "had sixty-five different ways to walk to the post office for his mail ... The old must search for the right mix of comfortable habits and new experiences. Without the former there is chaos; without the latter, there is ossification."

THE GOOD NEWS: OLDER PEOPLE ARE REJECTING SOCIETY'S MYTHS AND CREATING MEANINGFUL LIVES

Our potential to age with purpose and expectations has grown due to the marked improvements in the status and health of many older people. Many members of this group, which is unprecedented in numbers, wealth, and as a percent of the population, are willing to expend resources to achieve their preferences.

> *Nothing splendid has ever been achieved except by those who dared to believe that something inside them was superior to circumstances.*
> —Bruce Barton

Many are living longer, and the choices available to them during this extended life stage are increasing. Those who remain enthused about life can pursue a variety of active lifestyles. For instance, they can travel, engage in informal and formal studies, volunteer, and spend quality time with grown children, grandchildren, and friends.

> *Youth is happy because it has the ability to see beauty. Anyone who keeps the ability to see beauty never grows old.*
> —Franz Kafka

We can also choose to make extraordinary contributions in our older years. Some well-known people who have chosen to make their older years meaningful and productive were

> *I know of no more encouraging fact than the unquestionable ability of man to elevate his life by a conscious endeavor.*
> —Henry David Thoreau

noted in chapter two, but there are also many older people in our own communities who have created lives of meaning and purpose without fanfare or recognition. They cut across the demographic landscape, including the poor, the middle class, and the wealthy: every ethnicity, as well as people with disabilities. Most of us know such people. They are positive role models who can help us become more confident about creating our own visions, goals, and meaning.

STRATEGIES FOR DEVELOPING PURPOSES AND EXPECTATIONS

One of the tasks of aging identified by Carl Jung, and echoed by Victor Frankl and others, is to discover the meaning of life. We can choose to watch life go by or we can grow, develop, and become our full selves. But to grow and develop, we have to let go of perceptions of ourselves as we were at younger life stages and come to terms with our current realities. Holding on to our younger years is a losing battle in the end anyway. Just as with the story of Dorian Gray the denial of aging can lead to "being trapped forever in the body and spirit of youth without ever being able to mature or age." This is detrimental because "there are special human qualities and abilities that can only come to full blossom with age" (Dychtwald 1988, p. 343).

> *But if a man happens to find himself, he has a mansion which he can inhabit with dignity all the days of his life.*
> —James Michener

We need to confront our fixations with earlier life stages, our fears, habituations, and plateauing directly, so we can make the effort to create meaningful older lives. There are many ways that we can do this. Depending on your situation, some of the suggestions that follow may be more relevant than others for you. Strategies that can be employed are grouped under three headings: *our health, our attitudes*, and *our ability to plan and act.*

Our Health

We know that we need dependable cars to get from one place to another. Like our cars, our bodies are vehicles that need to be kept in good running order if we expect to have the energy to achieve our purposes. We need to take care of the one body we have been issued if we expect it to take care of us. Of course, genetics affect the dependability of our bodies, but they are also affected by the care we give them. As the results of the Harvard Study of Adult Development indicate, Valliant states (2002, p. 213), "Whether we live to a vigorous old age lies not so much in our stars or our genes as in ourselves."

A recent study of centenarians also provides support for the importance of maintaining our bodies. Subjects in this study lived past the age of one hundred mainly because they stayed healthy. In fact, even when they did get sick, they tended to bounce back faster than much younger individuals (Perls and Silver, 1999). This helps explain the fact that the average medical costs for patients who are centenarians are about 30 percent less than for patients between the ages of seventy and seventy-nine. While many of these centenarians had the good fortune to be born to healthy parents, most of them were also wise enough to capitalize on this kick-start by pursuing positive health practices: maintaining balanced diets, exercising, getting sufficient rest and sleep, managing stress well, and minimizing involvement with addictive habits like smoking or drinking alcoholic beverages.

> *Age only matters when one is aging. Now that I have arrived at a great age, I might just as well be twenty.*
> —Pablo Picasso

If the body is our vehicle, the mind is the steering mechanism that keeps the body on course. While there is evidence that brain cells die as we age, there is also evidence that we only use about 10 percent of our gray matter. There is a lot of room for mental stimulation and growth even with brain cell loss if we learn to exercise our brains and tap into even a small portion of the other 90 percent that is available for our use. In addition, the cell loss we do experience may not be as important as we thought. In fact, (Nuland, 1955, pp.55–56), "the higher intellectual areas of the cerebral cortex have a significantly lower degree of cell disappearance ... Recent research suggests that

> *The older I get the more clearly I remember the things that never happened.*
> —Mark Twain

certain cortical neurons seem actually to become more abundant after maturity." Further, even what appears to be declining mental abilities may actually be a purposeful process that helps us put a priority on long-term memory needs, which, in turn, supports the development of life's meaning. We may not exercise our short-term memory as much because we are occupied with clarifying and synthesizing the meaning of our lives (Hillman, 1999).

We need to exercise our minds as much as we need to exercise our bodies. We can do this in a variety of ways, including participating in formal and informal learning opportunities, being creative about how we go about our everyday activities, reducing rote and routine behaviors, pursuing challenging projects, engaging in stimulating conversations, and minimizing passive activities such as watching hours of mindless television.

> *I have enjoyed greatly the second blooming that comes ... It is as if a fresh sap of ideas and thoughts was rising in you.*
> —Agatha Christie

In the final analysis, most of us will find that our bodies become fragile before our minds do. In fact, we depend on our minds at least as much as on our bodies to arrive at the end of life's journey with understanding and meaning. It might even be argued that it is the withering away of our physical capacities that enables us to turn our energies inward and concentrate on the meaning of our lives.

> *In my old age there is a coming into flower. My body wanes; my mind waxes.*
> —Victor Hugo

Our Attitudes

Our attitudes shape our perceptions, which, in turn, become our reality as we experience it. Most of us have to cope with hardships and difficulties. How well we respond to these challenges has a lot to do with our attitudes. Do we focus on the positive

> *The proper function of man is to live, not to exist. I shall not waste my days trying to prolong them. I shall use my time.*
> —Jack London

and the possible or on the negative and the impossible? It is not whether we will have challenges; it is whether we have the attitudes that can help us respond to them effectively. Even as he was approaching his death, Morrie Schwartz was still able to say with conviction (Albom, 1997, p. 57), "I give myself a good cry if I need it. But then I concentrate on all the good things in my life."

Resilient people have positive attitudes because their self-feedback is positive. They focus on self-encouragement, support, forgiveness, and empowering themselves, and they concentrate on growth and development. However, before we can practice positive reinforcement and build our confidence, we may have to confront and reduce self-talk habits that interfere with our well-being. "I can't," "I won't," and "It's impossible" messages need to be replaced by "I can," "I will," and "It's possible" messages. Habits take time to form, and they are usually deeply held so they will probably also take time to change. The effort requires honesty, patience, and persistence, but it can be done!

> *There is only one way to get ready for immortality and that is to live this life and live it bravely and faithfully, and cheerfully as we can.*
> —Henry van Dyke

As we shift our attitudes toward the positive and the possible, we also need to focus more on the present and the future. As the saying goes, the past is prologue. The present is the only place we are, and the future is where we are going. Reviewing our past life is important. It can help us understand what our lives add up to, provide a foundation for living today, and a springboard for planning for the future. But we can't live in the past. What we experience now and will experience for whatever lifespan remains for us should be our main focus. We can only create purposes and expectations if we are willing to change and grow, and if we believe that there is potential for meaning in our older years.

> *It is only when we truly know and understand that we have a limited time on earth—and that we have no way of knowing when our time is up—that we will begin to live each day to the fullest, as if it was the only one we had.*
> —Elisabeth Kübler-Ross

Our Ability to Plan and Act

It is important to remain healthy and have positive attitudes, but unless we take actions that capitalize on these assets, we may still lead lives of quiet desperation. We create meaningful lives in our aging years by clarifying our priorities, setting goals, and making realistic plans.

- *A good starting place might be to engage in life review.* Write about your life with the intent of deriving meaning about what it adds up to so far, looking for clues about where it may be heading in the future.

> *One's own self is well hidden from one's own self: Of all mines of treasure, one's own is the last to be dug up.*
> —Friedrich Nietzche

- *Build on life review and reflect about the future.* Develop a mental vision about your preferred future. Ask yourself questions that help you create a vision about your future: Who will be in your life? What will you be doing? How will you be feeling physically and mentally? What challenges will you be dealing with? What will your purposes and expectations look like? Where will you live? And so on ...
- *Develop goals to help guide decision making and resource allocation.* Keep your goals clear and meaningful. They can help guide your actions for years to come.
- *Confirm your commitment to your goals and assess whether you are making progress in achieving them.* Do they really reflect your vision? Are they stated positively? Do they motivate you to explore possibilities and to live creatively? Can you measure whether you are accomplishing them? Be prepared to review and modify them if you think you are off course.

Once you have clarified your goals, actions. How we go about doing this depends on our priorities, our expectations, our personalities, and our resources. As we age, we need to use the limited amount of time left

> *Nothing must be postponed; find eternity in each moment.*
> —Henry David Thoreau

wisely and focus on activities that are challenging, meaningful, and move us toward our goals.

There are more options available now than ever before to help us create a meaningful aging life. Three options that increasing numbers of older people are choosing include *travel, learning, and giving*. Some of us may choose to focus on one of these options, but others may prefer to sample multiple options. What you decide should be based on relevance and meaning for you.

- *Travel to near and distant places.* Seeing the world and learning about different cultures can be an end in itself, but travel can also be a way of breaking out of routines, getting out of our comfort zones, and gaining the confidence to meet our goals. Some people make their own travel arrangements, either because they have limited resources or because they are adventurous and want to plan their journeys. Others, out of convenience or because they are not comfortable about managing their travel, prefer to select from the ever-growing number of specialized tours that are designed to meet the needs and interests of older people.

- *Information, knowledge, and wisdom through learning.* We live at a time of unprecedented opportunities for formal and informal learning experiences. We can pursue informal learning through such activities as reading, scanning the Web, hobbies, and discussions with others. We can also pursue traditional formal learning experiences, perhaps by enrolling in evening classes at a local school district, taking credit or noncredit courses, or even studying for a degree at a nearby university. There are also innovative formal learning options, including courses delivered by mail for study at home; Web-based courses and programs offered by an increasing number of universities; a wide variety of special programs for seniors on university campuses, including many universities that have created residential communities for elders that focus on learning, on or near campus; Elderhostel programs that offer opportunities to study a variety of topics all

> *Learn as if to live forever. Live as if to die tomorrow.*
> —Saying

around the world; or the do-it-yourself university approach pioneered by the University of the Third Age, which brings interested older people in a specific geographical area together to create and conduct their own learning experiences.

- **Giving to others.** When we reach our aging years, many of us focus on giving back in return for the many things that have been given to us. There are different ways to pursue this goal, including grand-parenting, mentoring, care-giving, philanthropy, and volunteering. When we give, we also receive in many ways. We get a feeling of well-being, a boost to our immune system, a deeper sense of meaning about our lives, and the chance to leave a legacy. We can only do these things if we stay true to our beliefs and make the lives of others better. As he prepared to die, Morrie Schwartz reminded us (Albom,, 1997, p. 174), "We can die without ever really going away. All the love you created is still there. You live on—in the hearts of everyone you have touched and nurtured while you were here."

> *Only a life lived for others is a life worthwhile.*
> —Albert Einstein

Exercise: Your Purposes and Expectations

This activity is intended to help you think about ways you can establish meaningful purposes and expectations.

1. Review the three strategic areas that support your ability to live with meaningful purposes and expectations that were described in the chapter. Assess your **current status** regarding your ability to apply them to promote purposes and expectations in your life. Circle your responses on the following five-point scale.

	Poor	1	2	3	4	5	Excellent
Your Health		1	2	3	4	5	
Your Attitudes		1	2	3	4	5	
Your Ability to Plan and Act		1	2	3	4	5	

2. Are there gaps between your current situation and your preferences? If so, how big are they? Which of the three areas concerns you the most?
3. Which ideas presented in the chapter do you think can help you reduce the gaps? List some that might be important for you to consider.

A.
B.
C.
D.
E.

The need to focus on meaning and create appropriate and challenging purposes is an important priority for those of us who want our aging years to be all they can be. Finding meaning is important to all of us. We can help each other as we focus on this important task. In fact, it might be helpful to share your hopes and concerns with others and encourage them to do the same with you. There is an important saying: "You have to do it yourself, but you don't have to do it alone."

> *Goal setting is the strongest force for human motivation.*
> —Don Clark

In Closing

Chapter 7 began with John's story. He intended to live a life of leisure when he retired, but he soon grew bored with endless rounds of golf and fishing trips. He realized that he needed to create a deeper meaning for his life or, like his father, he might go into a rapid downward spiral and die before his time. John knew he needed to reassess his idea of retirement. He was concerned that his life would be unsatisfactory if he didn't take action to change it.

He thought about how meaningful his life felt prior to retirement, when he was involved in a rich variety of activities and played important roles at work, in the community, and at home. He realized that he would have to do some serious thinking about what motivated him in the past and what he wanted his life to be like now and in the future. He decided he needed to develop activities that mattered to him if he was going to turn things around.

He began by engaging in life review activities, sorting through the pieces of his life. In the process, he identified what he wanted to do, and the adrenaline began to flow as he thought about his desire to travel and visit his family's homeland in France. He soon signed up for Elderhostel trips that were both educational and satisfied his curiosity about traveling to interesting places. He also volunteered as an assistant golf coach at the local high school, which let him tap into his golfing skills and his interest in mentoring and giving back. Besides, keeping up with teenagers was challenging and helped him stay in shape.

As he began to transform his vision and plans into actions, he felt more engaged with life. He even started keeping a journal. As a first entry, he listed his goals and his plans for actions. It wasn't long before the journal included reflections about how he was moving toward his goals and how excited and enthused he was about the activities he was pursuing.

Life was clearly becoming more interesting, but being a realist, he knew that conditions tend to change, and that interests shift. He decided he would have to revisit his goals and plans on a regular basis and be willing to modify them as needed. Realizing that he would need good role models, he also decided to connect with older, more experienced people who had created meaningful lives. Maybe, he thought, a few of them might even be willing to mentor him.

Chapter Eight

Meaningful Participation

I don't know what your destiny will be, but one thing I know: the only ones among you who will be really happy are those who will have sought and found how to serve.

—Albert Schweitzer

Carol was in her late sixties and reasonably healthy, but something was clearly missing in her life. She felt alone, disconnected, and unable to find adequate outlets for her considerable energies. After working more than forty years, she had recently stepped down as president of the successful job placement company she'd created. For the most part, as she looked back on her career, she was left with a feeling of fulfillment and a strong sense of self-worth. She'd loved her work, which was challenging and put her in frequent contact with many people who valued her information and support. In fact, her contacts extended well beyond her employees and customers. She also participated in a variety of business-related organizations, including the local chamber of commerce. She left the company in capable hands and vowed not to interfere or even to look back. It was time to move on, leave her past life, and build a new one that would be right for her in retirement. The trouble was that she didn't know how to do this. She had worked hard right up to the end of her career, assuming that things would fall in place easily after she retired. She enjoyed the flexibility and freedom she was experiencing, but she soon came to miss the satisfaction and sense of well-being she got when she worked with others on company activities. If she was going to develop a meaningful life, she needed to find new ways to participate meaningfully and develop positive outlets for her energies.

Carol was fully engaged with challenging and important activities during her working years. She knew some adjustments would have to be made as she moved into retirement, but she was sure that she could overcome any obstacles that might stand in the way of a satisfying older life. After all, she had more than adequately met the challenges that came her way as a teenager, as a young adult, and as a businessperson.

Now, as she thought back over the years, she realized that choices she made earlier might have contributed to her current state of dissatisfaction. First, although there were offers of marriage, she had consciously decided to remain single so she could devote her energies to her growing company. Second, she had lost touch with her extended family. In fact, she didn't even see her siblings or their children frequently because she was so busy running her company. Third, she had participated heavily in groups and organizations, but these connections were all work related and, for the most part, were no longer of much interest to her. Fourth, she'd never seemed to have the time during her working years to cultivate other activities she was interested in, like ballroom dancing, photography, and gardening. Neither did she have the time to participate in community activities, let alone volunteer for neighborhood, community, state, or national improvement efforts.

If she was going to live a vital older life, Carol knew that she needed to feel challenged, and she would need to reach out and participate with others. But, like many of us, she was unsure of how to go about doing this. What she did know was that there was a large gap between the highly successful and full life she'd experienced in the past and what she was going through now. She knew what the rules of the game were earlier in life, but she wasn't at all sure of what she now had to do to approximate the quality of the life she'd led before retirement.

Chapter 8 examines how important meaningful participation is if we expect to live with vitality and enthusiasm as we age. It also explores why it is so difficult for many of us to find ways of participating meaningfully, and it suggests strategies that can help us overcome these barriers.

Meaningful Participation: Why Is It So Important?

Meaningful participation can lead to a sense of belonging and relevance. Doing so with families, friends, groups and organizations, as well as within our broader communities, reminds us that we are part of something bigger than ourselves. It also nurtures us and provides us with the means to nurture those who nurture us.

There is no simple way to describe what meaningful participation looks like because it can take many different forms. For example, it might be:

- Belonging to social clubs;
- Engaging in civic affairs;
- Relating intergenerationally with our adult children and grandchildren;
- Networking with friends and others who share similar interests;
- Volunteering in our communities; or
- Participating in adult learning experiences

Meaningful participation is more likely to be part of our lives if we are also able to go inward and reflect. As we synthesize our lives, we promote our growth and extend our ability to give to others. Reflection is vitally important at this stage of life, which is a period that Erikson (1986) refers to as the "Age of Integrity." Typically emerging in our sixties, this is a time when we can realize our potential for growth, or we can despair and become stuck in place. We can become wiser, more tolerant, and more patient and open-minded, or we can deteriorate, becoming depressed and set in our ways. There is truth in the old saying that we are either growing or we are dying!

Most of us seek to balance time for solitude and reflection with time to connect and participate, but regardless of where our individual balance points may be, to one degree or another, we all need to reach out, network, and participate. Through participation, we discover outlets for our energies and creativity, gain a sense of belonging, and realize our self-worth. We feel like we are part of something bigger than ourselves, and as a result, we are likely to feel more fulfilled and enthused about our lives.

Connectivity and participation can have a positive impact on our health and longevity. Those who have ongoing relationships—married,

> *I have always had a dread of becoming a passenger in life.*
> —Princess Margrethe of Denmark

churchgoers, caring friends and groups that nurture us—are more likely to stay healthy and live longer. It is not just *being* with others; it is *participation* that makes the difference.

As human beings, we need to connect with other people. This need will not go away as we age. In fact, during our older years we become less concerned about acquiring material things and more interested in developing and maintaining relationships. This drive can be expressed in a variety of ways. For example, we might choose to:

- socialize more with friends
- stay in touch with extended families
- spend quality time with adult children and grandchildren
- engage in adult learning activities that bring us into close contact with other learners and seekers
- become involved in civic affairs
- provide time, care, and support for those in need, including caring for aging people who have disabilities, helping youngsters who need love and support, and engaging in community improvement activities

Exercise: What Meaningful Participation Means to You

Meaningful participation is about being involved in ways that leave us with a sense of belonging and relevance. When were the times that you participated in ways that led to a sense of belonging and relevance?

1. As you think back over your life, list situations when you felt like you were participating meaningfully. Also, try to capture what it was about these situations that left you feeling that way.

   A.
   B.
   C.
   D.

2. Can you identify some common themes that cut across these situations?

   A.
   B.
   C.

3. Are these themes still important to you? If so, are they still part of your life?

4. Are there other themes regarding relevance and belonging that seem to be emerging for you? If so, what do you think you need to do make them part of your life?

BARRIERS TO MEANINGFUL PARTICIPATION

Meaningful participation means different things to different people. But there is a common thread: We seek to participate in ways that support our desire to create and maintain lives marked by belonging and relevance. This is difficult to achieve at any stage of life, but it is particularly challenging during our older years, in part because of society's *negative beliefs* about aging and, too often, our own self-defeating *perceptions and behaviors.*

Negative Beliefs

In chapter two, we explored how much beliefs about aging and older people have shifted over the past few centuries. In the eighteenth century, older people were revered. In part, this was because there were so few of them, but it was also because they controlled society's wealth. Remaining centrally engaged in the economic system, many older people accumulated land and wealth and worked until they were incapacitated or died.

This is no longer the case. Beginning with the last half of the nineteenth century, there was a shift from agrarian to industrialized economies in many Western countries. Many people moved from small rural towns to large urban cities. As the Industrial Revolution took hold, bureaucratic rules proliferated to make the roles, relationships, and expectations of workers more predictable. In short order, we began to be identified by the roles we play to earn a living more than by how we participate with our families and our communities.

People who at earlier times might have been engaged in independent, meaningful, and respected work in the past—such as, for example, farmers or artisans—are now mostly employed by large and often impersonal organizations. As this change took hold, the concept of retirement has become pervasive. The organizations we work for define our self-worth by setting rules about when we must stop working. Because many of us define ourselves closely with our work roles, our sense of belonging and relevance are threatened when we retire and move into our aging years.

Changes in our economic structure and the changing beliefs about aging that have accompanied them are deeply embedded in our culture. These beliefs may not be conscious, but they affect perceptions and behaviors in pervasive ways. The longer they persist, the more they are assumed to be true. Some beliefs that

> *Rage, rage against the night, against the dying light.*
> —Dylan Thomas

have become barriers to meaningful participation in our older years include the following:

- ***Older people have little to contribute.*** As Erikson states (1986, p. 298), we have relegated aging people "to the onlooker bleachers of our society, we have classified them as unproductive, inadequate, and inferior." Older people have more life experiences to share and usually have time to give in meaningful ways, but they are not frequently invited to participate, even as volunteers. Even when they do participate, their ability to contribute effectively is limited because their unique skills and knowledge aren't usually taken into account. The dominant belief is that older people are not interested or able to contribute effectively. If we are not taken seriously when we seek to participate, it is easy for us to conclude that we are not regarded as potential contributors and we probably can't make a difference anyway.

  > *Intelligence, reflection, and judgment reside in old men, and if there had been none of them, no states could exist at all.*
  > —Cicero

- ***Younger people aren't usually comfortable being with older people.*** They have been conditioned to stereotype older peoples' behaviors in ways that make it undesirable to spend time with them. For example, they tend to believe that older people repeat themselves frequently, are forgetful, and make unreasonable demands for help and support. As a result, many of them would rather buy presents for older people than share time with them. Blinded by negative stereotypes, many younger people, including our own grown children, are not often aware of the urgent need of aging people to participate in meaningful activities.

- ***Western religions emphasize the importance of the afterlife over the value of older life on Earth.*** Western religions, including Christianity, Judaism, and Islam, teach that life is the time when we prepare for an afterlife in heaven. Emphasis is placed on preparing to meet our maker and for an eternal life in heaven more than it is on meaningful participation in

our aging years (Shachter-Shalomi, 1995). However, it is also important to note that, despite these beliefs, these same religions do provide numerous opportunities for members to participate meaningfully in activities related to their chosen religion. For example, they are encouraged to assist at services, teach Sunday school, join committees, and participate in social groups.
- To underscore how much our beliefs are culturally based, we need only take a cursory look at other societies in which older people are granted higher regard and status. Anthropologists and other social scientists provide numerous examples of societies as diverse as the Fiji Islands, Colombia, Israel, and Germany, which honor older people and have developed relevant and important roles for them to play, including being wise elders, arbiters of conflicts, and keepers of the culture (Friedan, 1993).

On Okinawa, elders continue to work a few hours daily, right up to their final days, and younger Okinawans encourage and support them in their efforts to do so. As Pipher (1999, p. 43) points out, "Many people live to be more than a hundred and stay in remarkably good health. There is little cancer, diabetes, osteoporosis, or strokes among people who stay on the island, but if they move away, they have the same mortality rates as others." These societies, unlike ours, recognize that setting aside roles carried in younger years does not mean that we should disengage from society. Rather, they view the aging years as a transition time, a time when we move on and search out more appropriate age-related ways of participating.

Our Perceptions and Our Behaviors

Our sense of who we are can support or detract from our ability to engage in meaningful participation as we age. For example, how do you respond to the following questions?

1. Do you seek out new friends or do you just stick with your tried and true old friends? We meet the world halfway or we stay within our comfort zone and only interact with people we know. Remember the story about the old friends who know each other's jokes so well that they give them numbers? That

Resilient Aging

way they can save time when they tell them to each other, over and over! Old friends are wonderful. They provide us with a sense of belonging, but we also need new stimulation and new people in our lives to feel fully alive.

2. Do you behave in ways that make others feel negative about you? For example, do you act frumpy and grumpy, repeat stories, criticize a lot, and talk more than you listen? Do you use language that dates you? Our behaviors send messages to others. What kind of messages do you send?

> *It is as hard to see one's self as to look backwards without turning around.*
> —Henry David Thoreau

3. Do you expect your children to take care of you? Do you try to live vicariously through them? They have their own challenges to deal with. Neither they nor we are likely to respond to our challenges effectively if we lean on them too heavily for support. Such expectations can lead to dysfunctional relationships or maybe even being cut off from our own offspring.

4. Do you believe that unpaid work is as valuable as paid work? Do you try to find ways to give back to others? Do you volunteer to help those who may not be as independent and capable as you are? Giving can be as rewarding to ourselves as it is to those we help.

If we behave in negative ways, are unwilling to extend our relationships, expect to be taken care of by our adult children, and don't support others, we will probably find ourselves isolated and depleted. If we continue to behave in this way, we are susceptible to manifestations of *learned helplessness*, the pessimistic belief that we can't improve our situations (Seligman 1990). However, if we are willing and able to behave in ways that make others want to interact with us, maintain a balanced and healthy relationship with our own adult children, and value and help

> *Habit is ... not to be flung out the window by any man, but coaxed downstairs a step at a time.*
> —Mark Twain

others, we will be on our way to meaningful participation. People who take this positive approach recognize that there is no such thing as entitlement. Support must be earned repeatedly. They manifest *learned optimism,* the belief that they can learn from life's challenges and grow and develop in healthy ways.

STRATEGIES THAT PROMOTE MEANINGFUL PARTICIPATION

As we age, we have to let go of well-known work and family roles that are no longer appropriate. But letting go is only half the story: As we let go of old roles, the challenge is to redefine ourselves, take on new roles, clarify what truly matters to us, and pursue activities that promote belonging and relevance. To do so, we need to focus on two priorities that

> *The great use of life is to spend it for something that will outlast us.*
> —William James

emerge at this life stage: being *generative,* or giving and receiving care and support, and having *integrity,* synthesizing our lives and sharing our wisdom (Erikson, 1994). If we don't find ways of pursuing generative and integrity, we are likely to turn inward and experience despair and regret.

We need to feel that we belong and that we are relevant, but this can be a challenge in a society like ours, which does not often recognize, let alone support, the needs of older people to participate. Given this situation, we need to take it upon ourselves to develop meaningful outlets for participation. We each have our own unique personalities, life experiences, abilities, and skills, so we must each generate our own strategies to achieve meaningful participation. However, there are some basic strategies that can be helpful to all of us if adapted to our own situations: ***positive attitudes, social networks, a balance between reaching out and turning inward, giving, and developing supportive environments.***

Positive Attitudes

An active and energized nursing home resident put it succinctly (Kidder, 1993, p. 197–98): "Life itself won't give you joy unless you will it. What life does give is time and space. It's up to you to fill it." In other words, our attitudes and behaviors create our realities. The clearer we are about our attitudes and why we hold them, the more aware we become of how much they impact our lives.

> *What lies behind us and what lies before us are small matters compared to what lies within us.*
> —Ralph Waldo Emerson

That is the first step. The next step is to modify those attitudes that are dysfunctional and bolster those that support meaningful participation. Among other things, attitude modification is about realizing that we no longer are in the work-related roles we played before we retired. Thinking and behaving in ways that were required in our former roles may no longer be relevant. Instead, we can openly seek help, support others, and be genuinely affectionate and caring. If we let go of old roles and come to peace with the loss of whatever authority and status we might once have had, we can create meaning based on who we are now. The benefits of making the shift can be great, but to do so, we need to pay attention, be flexible, and learn to relate in ways that promote belonging and relevance.

Social Networks

Extroverts prefer spending time in the company of others, while introverts prefer having extensive time being alone. However, to one degree or another, all of us have the need to socialize with others for friendship and support. Positive relationships add to the meaningfulness of our lives, lead to greater vitality and a sense of well-being, and remind us that we have a place in the bigger picture of things.

When we have a good level of support, we tend to assume it will always be there. However, we should not take it for granted because things may change. It is easier to attract support and intimacy when we are healthy and engaged with life than when we are disabled or depressed. Taking time to nurture and expand our connections while we are feeling good about things can be well worth the effort.

Participating with others who are part of our own age cohort is important. We need to share stories and be in the company of people at our life stage, those who can understand what we are talking about. We need to maintain the relationships we have already developed, but it is also important to expand our social networks. If we only socialize with our own age group, we limit our opportunities for growth and development. Our conversations will likely focus on the past, health issues, and our mortality. In fact, those who only interact with other aging people tend to be less engaged in life, lonelier, less satisfied, and, most important, less healthy than people who seek out relationships across the generations (Friedan, 1993).

When we include people from other life stages in our social networks, we increase our opportunities to experience a wider scope of sharing and to give and receive support. Older positive aging role models can help us discover ways to live resiliently, while younger people who are curious about their futures as aging people can provide outlets for us to provide support, practice being generative, and leave a legacy.

Our most important intergenerational network is the one we can create with our family, particularly with our adult children and grandchildren. When we raise children and watch them grow into productive and positive adults, we can take pride in our achievements. With the arrival of grandchildren, we can get a deepening sense of our procreativity and the importance of our elder role, which includes passing on traditions and telling stories that bind the family's generations together.

A Balance between Reaching Out and Turning Inward to Reflect

Life is a perpetual balancing act. We need to go inward and reflect to take care of our inner selves, but we also need to reach outward, participate, and give to others. As we age, we have more freedom to choose whether and how we participate, but we also have the need for solitude and reflection so we can integrate and synthesize our lives. The challenge is to balance our

> *To live fully outwardly and inwardly, not to ignore external reality for the sake of the inner life, or the reverse—that's quite a task.*
> —Etty Hillesum

inherent drive to participate with our need to go inward. That is, we need to give and receive support, but we also need to reflect and clarify life's meaning and purpose.

President Carter is a great example of someone who maintained a balance between reaching out and turning inward. After leaving the White House, he took on activities that were meaningful, like creating Habitat for Humanity, a program that brings volunteers together to build homes for needy people, and he has traveled to other countries to monitor contested elections. However, recognizing the need to reflect and grow as an aging person, he has also chosen to scale back the scope of his activities. He has maintained responsibilities that are still appropriate and has relinquished others that can be assumed effectively by younger people. Rebalancing like this can work well, for both those who relinquish responsibilities and those who assume them. It provides older individuals with the time and solitude to reflect about their lives and helps younger people move into active roles that are appropriate for their life stage.

Giving

Nurturing others can be rewarding for those who give as well as for those who receive. We feel good when we give to others. In fact, we may even experience a boost to our immune system when we do so. As Rabbi Hillel said, "If am not for myself, who will be? And if I am only for myself, what am I? And if not now, when?" Giving helps us achieve meaning for our lives.

> *Enhance the humanity of the other, because in that process, you enhance your own.*
> — Desmond Tutu

> *Example is not the main thing in influencing others. It is the only thing.*
> —Albert Schweitzer

Maggie Kuhn, the founder of the Gray Panthers, says elders have the potential to play five giving roles. They can be any of the following:

- *Mentors* who guide the young
- *Mediators* who help society get through civil and racial conflicts
- *Monitors* who act as watchdogs over local, state, and national policy makers
- *Mobilizers* who promote important social changes
- *Motivators* who encourage people to balance self-interests with the public good

A powerful way to experience these "M" roles is through volunteering. In the United States, ninety-three million citizens volunteer about 20 billion hours of their time annually. This translates to about one of every three Americans volunteering, on average, 220 hours per year.

Older citizens volunteered at the same rate as the general population, but they only provided about 150–200 hours annually, or about 3 or 4 hours of time a week (Perls and Silver, 1999). Given the time that is available to them, older people are relatively underutilized as volunteers. Many are interested in participating in efforts to improve society but often report that it is difficult for them to find ways to do so. It is important that we find ways for people to volunteer at this life stage because it is a win-win situation: Society can tap into a deep pool of talent and energy, and those who volunteer can fulfill their desire to give back and leave a legacy. It is in everyone's best interests to increase the number of older volunteers as well as the amount of time they help. Older volunteers can, for example, volunteer their talents and energies as follows:

> *Almost anything you do will be insignificant, but it is very important that you do it.*
> — Mohandas Gandhi

> *Life is like a stone, skipping over clear water. You don't know how many skips you're going to get or for how long. What's important are the ripples you make and how they affect the ones around you.*
> —Donnie Christensen

- **Helping other older people who need support.** This might take the form of delivering Meals on Wheels, visiting shut-ins, doing hospice work, sharing skills and knowledge at a local senior center, and driving those in need of a ride to get to doctor's appointments, go shopping, or attend church.

> *Do all the good you can, by all the means you can, in all the ways you can, in all the places you can, at all the times you can, to all the people you can, as long as ever you can.*
> —John Wesley

- ***Becoming surrogate grandparents.*** We don't have to have grandchildren to experience being a grand parent. We can have positive experiences and leave a powerful legacy behind if we volunteer to be surrogate grandparents for children who either don't have any grandparents or whose grandparents don't live nearby. Surrogate grand parenting programs provide elders with a powerful sense of belonging, while giving children the nurturance they need.
- **Mobilizing support for policies that can improve people's lives.** The growing number of older people places this group in the strategic position to make positive differences in the public arena. Older citizens have extensive and varied life experiences, the desire to leave a legacy, and the time and motivation to focus on creating needed changes and improvements. In part, this life stage group has a lot of clout simply because it takes voting seriously. In fact, this age group votes at a higher rate than any other age group: For example, in the 2000 election in the United States, two-thirds of the older population voted, compared to 44 percent of those in the twenty-five to thirty-four age group and only about 25 percent of those in the twenty-one to twenty-four age group. But their influence is also felt because many are politically active, believing that they can achieve much for the general population as well as for themselves when they join together. For example, the American Association of Retired People has successfully protested cuts made in prenatal and child health-care programs at the same time that it has argued for the maintenance and expansion of Medicare. The Gray Panthers have demanded justice in areas as diverse as representation of African Americans in Congress; exposure of hearing aid scams; health care for everyone; amendments to the Television Code of Ethics to make age as legitimate an area of concern as race and sex; and promoted legislation to raise the mandatory retirement age from sixty-five to seventy. Besides becoming involved in such national initiatives, there are countless opportunities for aging people to organize and make a difference in their own communities. For example, they can press for needed changes and improvements in the public schools, as well as in local and regional governments.

Mike M. Milstein

Developing Supportive Environments

The environments we live in—our neighborhoods, communities, towns, cities, and countries—can impact our well-being, either negatively or positively. If they are supportive and inviting, they enhance our sense of belonging and relevance. If they aren't, we will be left with the feeling that we are irrelevant and that we do not belong.

If we live in negative environments, we can sit back and wait and hope for things to change, or we can take the initiative to develop and shape things in ways that promote and encourage older adult participation in meaningful ways. The current elder generation and the boomer group that is joining it have had extensive life experiences in shaping supportive environments. For example, in the United States, members of the baby boomer generation became adults in the Kennedy years and participated in the Civil Rights movement and the debates and struggles over the Vietnam War. They proved their ability to impact changes locally and nationally then, and there is every reason to believe they will continue to do so in the future.

> *There also comes with age a gradually increasing capacity to contribute to society.*
> —Abraham Kaplan

We get direct personal benefits when we create supportive environments. As we push our boundaries and take risks, our potential to grow and develop is enhanced. We also are more confident of being able to take care of ourselves as we increase the potential for more equitable giving and receiving relationships with our children, friends, and others.

Whether we are in good health or disabled, there are things we can do on our own and together to create environments that are more positive. For example, those who are in good health can take the initiative to create neighborhood gardens and coordinate the redevelopment of neglected communities. Those who are disabled might choose to create a family tree or to motivate adult children and grandchildren to create a family newspaper. The point is that, regardless of our situations, we can find ways to belong and promote our relevance as individuals and as an older population.

Technological advances make it even more possible to participate meaningfully, regardless of our particular state of health. For example, the Internet can bring the knowledge of the world into our homes. E-mail can let us share our thoughts and feelings with family members and friends, regardless of where they live. We can share what we see by downloading digital photographs into our computers and sending them to our friends and our family. We can even connect through our computers for visual and voice sessions across great distances. Mobile phones and low-cost long-distance systems further expand our ability to stay in touch. Undoubtedly, many other technological innovations will be created that will make it easier to engage in meaningful participation.

Margaret Mead has observed, "Never doubt that small groups of thoughtful, committed citizens can change the world. Indeed, it is the only thing that ever has." This observation sums it up. When we come together and share our energies and abilities, we have the potential to make a difference. We can make our lives and the lives of others more meaningful while we shape a world that understands, cares, and supports our growth and development.

Mike M. Milstein

Exercise: You and Meaningful Participation

This activity is intended to help you think about strategies that you may want to focus on to increase meaningful participation in your life. Review the five strategies introduced in chapter 8. Assess your current ability to apply them in order to achieve meaningful participation in your life. Circle your responses on the following five-point scale:

	Underdeveloped	1	2	3	4	5	*Highly Developed*
Positive Attitudes		1	2	3	4	5	
Networking and Socializing		1	2	3	4	5	
Reaching out While Turning Inward		1	2	3	4	5	
Giving		1	2	3	4	5	
Developing Supportive Environments		1	2	3	4	5	

1. Are there gaps between your current situation and your preferences? Which of the five strategies have the biggest gaps?

2. To reduce these gaps, what specific ideas presented in chapter 8 do you think are important to consider?

IN CLOSING

Chapter 8 began with the story of Carol, who felt at loose ends after leaving a successful career. She was busy before she retired and hadn't given much thought to how she would be spending her older years. As a result, she went from being a centrally important player in her work role to feeling marginalized. She needed to find positive ways to participate meaningfully during her retirement years. She knew she would be an unhappy person if she did nothing to change her situation. Reflecting about the many positive and exciting times she'd experienced through her work, she realized that her knowledge and skills could prove to be useful in her efforts to overcome the difficulties she was encountering.

She realized that the first thing she needed to focus on was an attitude adjustment. In particular, she needed to stop sending herself "poor me" messages. It would be helpful if she could create new relationships so she would feel connected, She figured that a good way to do so might be to engage in compassionate service efforts that allowed her to focus her many talents on community improvement activities. She was delighted when the chamber of commerce asked her to help facilitate its efforts to identify and train new leaders for civic and private organizations. In short order, she made the necessary connections and became involved. This activity gave others the opportunity to learn good business practices from her considerable experience and knowledge. Just as important, she found that doing so made her feel good.

She also focused on developing a new social network to compensate for the loss of the relationships that had been readily available through her work activities. She began by spending more time with her nieces and nephews and mentoring young people who were interested in the business world. She also participated in community-based meetings and programs geared to the interests of older people, which provided a more solid foundation for her new life stage, giving her the important opportunity to meet others who were dealing with similar issues. It wasn't long before she and other retired people she was becoming acquainted with began to provide support for each other in the form of advice, transportation when there was need for such help, and simply being available as caring listeners.

Carol also decided to pursue interests she had set aside when she was too busy during her working years. She started to take ballroom dancing lessons, signed up for photography classes in the local school district's evening program, and joined a local gardening club. It wasn't long before she thought she would have to make some hard choices about which interests to pursue because there just wasn't enough time to do everything she wanted to do!

Carol was turning the corner. She was becoming involved and feeling as if she belonged and was truly relevant to others around her. She even started coaching friends who were going to retire soon, hoping that doing so might make their transitions more understandable and smoother.

Chapter Nine
Putting It All Together

Life is what we make it, always has been, always will be.
—Grandma Moses

At the outset of the book, some questions were raised for your consideration: How much do you know about aging? Do you have the information you need to prepare for your own aging years? Do you think that you can age with energy, enthusiasm, and wellness? Or, on the contrary, do you think that aging will be a time of decline, disease, and destitution? Do you even give much forethought to your aging years, or is the prospect so negative that you avoid thinking about it as much as possible?

The fact that you are reading this book probably means that you *are* thinking about your aging years. It also probably means that you don't assume that aging has to be a negative experience. In fact, it is my hope that the resiliency concepts and strategies presented in the book have enhanced your confidence that you can indeed age with energy, enthusiasm, and wellness.

> *To know how to grow old is the master-work of wisdom, and one of the most difficult chapters in the great art of living.*
> —Henri Amiel

We all want to age resiliently, but there is no single blueprint for doing so because each of us is unique. The strategies explored in the book are a cafeteria of ideas that can be selectively called on to help you create your own unique design for aging well. That's

> *I always plan for the future. When the time comes, if the plan is here and I'm not, it's no problem. But if I'm here and the plan isn't, that's a problem.*
> —Anonymous senior citizen

the purpose of this final chapter: to help sharpen your thinking about your plans for aging resiliently.

To be able to create our plans, we need to reflect and develop a vision of what we mean by a resilient older life.   It might be of help if I briefly summarize my own reflections about planning to age with resilience. In particular, I want to emphasize how the six resiliency elements explored in the book have become the foundation of how I am responding to these challenging times. Then we will turn to specific ideas that you might want to consider as you work on your own meaningful design for aging resiliently.

How I Have Applied Resiliency Elements

In chapter 1, I described my experiences as I prepared for and moved through the first few years of retirement. I talked about:

- The very different ways my grandfather and father dealt with retirement, and how their contrasting approaches helped me realize the importance of staying active and energized in my older years.
- How deeply involved I was in my work as a professor and my concerns about whether I would be able to let go of that life when I retired.
- The absence of information or support from my university regarding the psychological and spiritual aspects of retirement.
- Having to renegotiate my relationship with my wife when I retired and she continued to work a few more years before she also retired.
- The need to sort through and prioritize my non-work activities and hobbies.

I also shared some important questions that were on my mind as I thought about retirement: What will it be like? Will I feel the same sense of purpose and challenge that I had felt throughout my career? Will I continue

> *If you don't know where you are going, you will probably end up somewhere else.*
> —Lawrence J. Peter

to be part of a community of caring people? Will I remain healthy? Will I live a full life until I die? How will I face my own mortality?

Slowly, a sense of a meaningful older life began to take shape in my mind. I started to keep a journal to capture my thoughts and concerns. Because it sums up my beliefs about life as I age, I would like to share a particular entry with you:

> A meaningful life is like a good soup. We need to add spices to soup stock. The basic ingredients are in the stock, but they don't take on a distinctive character or flavor without the spices. I need spice in my life in much the same way that the soup stock needs them. Learning to age well means figuring out how to get the right spices into the soup!

As I prepared for retirement, the vision of what I wanted it to be like started to emerge. Reflecting on the questions that I had posed, I realized that I would need to avoid making any assumptions about life continuing as it had before retirement; sort out, inventory, and synthesize my passage from birth to retirement; and clarify what I want my life to be like in the near and long-term future. I stayed focused on the questions and guidelines I posed as I transitioned into retirement. In fact, I developed a to-do list to help me keep my focus on aging with resilience. I decided I would need to:

> *How can we live without our lives? How will we know it is ours without our past?*
> — John Steinbeck

- Chip away at old habits that would keep me in a comfort zone but could become barriers to growth opportunities.
- Explore opportunities to be an amateur, or a learner, and resist the pull to remain the "expert," knowing more and more about less and less, that I had become over my many years as a professor.

> *Obstinate habits do not disappear until replaced by other habits.*
> —Carl Jung

- Reflect on my reflections to sort out how I wanted my life to proceed. To do this would require that I resist viewing "doing" as productive and daydreaming, conceptualizing, and synthesizing as nonproductive.

- Become more comfortable about being on the journey and not obsessing about the destination. I can't put too much emphasis on a place to be reached. My desire to know where I am going is okay, but it can also get in the way of the journey. I've got to trust the process and let go of my need for control.

It has been challenging to stay true to these guidelines. However, while I still have a long way to go, I am making progress in shaping a resilient older life for myself. For example, I have:

Learned to let go of my work role and my university life. I no longer look back to see how "they" are doing without me.

> *There is nothing, absolutely nothing, a man cannot forget except himself, his own character.*
> —Arthur Shopenhauer

- Learned how to apply skills acquired during my career that support my emerging interests and passions. I still consult, present workshops, and write, but now I focus these activities on the aging process, and I limit the amount of time I spend on them.
- Coped well with two crises since I retired—the challenge of prostate cancer and the loss of my son. I believe I would have had a much more difficult time getting through these challenges without openness to spirituality and a broadening perspective about the meaning of life.

Focused on minimizing old habits that are no longer useful, modifying others that are still functional, and developing new ones that support my well-being.

What does all this have to do with being resilient? As I look back over the early years of my retirement, I can see how the six resiliency elements and the strategies that promote them have become a daily part of my experience.

> *Vision without action is merely a dream.*
> —Joel Barker

Positive Connections. I am increasingly aware of the need to develop and maintain healthy, supportive, and positive connections. In part, I have focused on enriching connections that were formed prior to my retirement, like those with family, friends, and my men's support group. But I have also developed connections with others who have recently moved into retirement, and I have expanded the intergenerational connections I have with people who are both older and younger than I am.

Clear, Consistent, and Appropriate Boundaries. Expectations that guide my behaviors have changed significantly since I retired. Of particular importance is the fact that my life is no longer ruled by university role requirements or institutional expectations. I have become acutely aware of the need to replace these externally driven boundaries with my own internally created boundaries. For example, I have developed daily routines that fit my new life rhythms, including regular times for sleeping, waking, mealtimes, and home maintenance activities. I have also made efforts to stay in touch with family and friends, and I have set aside regular time for writing, hobbies, and volunteer activities. These self-defined expectations have helped me avoid anomie, the sense of running down or dislocation. New rhythms have been emerging to replace the rhythms that I left behind when I retired.

Life-Guiding Skills. Many of the goal-setting, conflict management, problem-solving, and decision-making skills that I developed over a lifetime are proving to be highly useful in retirement, but they have needed to be honed down. I was an "expert" in dealing with my challenges as a professor and as a family man because I had a lot of experience in these arenas, and they had become predictable. Now I am an amateur again. I am discovering that I need to modify and expand upon my skills to meet new challenges. For example, I have had to develop new goals, modify basic skills to fit my changing status and age, and solve unique problems associated with my growing interest in cooking, photography, gardening, and competitive croquet. I have also had to become informed about the challenges and possibilities of my aging years. In this regard, I am applying things I've learned from books and articles I have collected, which deal with older people's health concerns, dietary needs, and exercise options such as yoga and tai chi. I have also been learning and applying information about my interest in creativity and spirituality.

> *Have a plan—and a plan B.*
> —Kirby Puckett

Nurture and Support. My work as a professor brought me into close contact with many interesting people. I had many varied and positive interactions with students, faculty, and community members, some of which have evolved into caring relationships. However, retirement, by necessity, meant a loss of many of the regular interactions that fueled these relationships. I have made efforts to maintain those I can,

> *Kindness in words creates confidence. Kindness in thinking creates profoundness. Kindness in giving creates love.*
> —Lao-Tzu

replace those I can't, and develop others that are meaningful to me. For example, as noted, I have prioritized the time that my wife and I spend together. I am also trying to connect with my daughter more frequently and reach out to my friends when they are in need of support. I am making conscious efforts to enhance my intergenerational connections by supporting the few remaining family members from my parents' generation and mentoring and learning from my daughter's friends. I am also engaging in many voluntary activities. When I do, I find that I receive at least as much as I give.

> *How dull it is to pause, to make an end, to rust unburnished, not to shine in use! As though to breathe were life!*
> —Tennyson

Purposes and Expectations. I needed to think about the meaning of my life when I retired. The purposes and expectations of my work life were no longer relevant. I had to create new definitions of what was important to me. I found a powerful source of meaning when I began to focus on understanding the aging process and sharing what I learned about it with others. I was fortunate because the knowledge and skills I had accumulated about promoting resiliency in schools during my working years proved useful as I started exploring resilient aging. In addition, I have become intrigued with spirituality, as well as how it relates to my own growth and development.

Meaningful Participation. My career provided extensive opportunities to participate in challenging activities at the university, in schools, and in the community. However, because most of these activities are no longer a part of my life, I have had to find others to replace them. It has been a slow rebuilding effort, but I have been discovering new ways to reach out and participate meaningfully. For example, I have maintained some consulting activities, helped to create a support group that is interested in the aging process, become involved in an advisory capacity at local senior centers, and made presentations and led workshops about resilient aging. I have helped organize several extended family get-togethers that have renewed and deepened supportive family relationships. I have also joined a local choir and enrolled in continuing education classes, in part to gain new knowledge, but also as a way of meeting and participating with interesting people.

Resilient Living in Your Older Years

As you may have noticed, many of the strategies that I talked about in my retirement story cut across a number of resiliency elements. For example, involvement with friends and family members has been important to me in developing positive connections, clarifying boundaries, seeking nurturance and support, and participating meaningfully. In other words resiliency strategies serve more than one quality-of-life need. Life is not like a layer cake, composed of neat and tidy layers. Rather, it is more like a marble cake: the features may still be recognizable, but they are blended and mixed throughout.

The choice is ours. We can grow or decline in our aging years, depending on how willing we are to exercise our resiliency muscles. For example, it is certainly a major challenge to cope with insufficient finances, health problems, and the loss of loved ones. But even in these situations, there is still much that we can do to improve the quality of our lives, *if we are willing to do so*. For example:

> *The biggest temptation is to settle for too little.*
> —Thomas Merton

- ***Financial resources*:** As individuals, we don't have much influence over economic downturns in the marketplace, but we do have the ability to choose whether and how to invest our resources; we can control our spending habits; and we can take joy in the many things that are inexpensive or free, like being in nature, listening to beautiful music, and visiting museums.

- **Health:** We may have little choice about whether we will have to cope with genetically related diseases such as diabetes. But even if we encounter such genetic health issues, we can have a positive impact on the situation. For example, by exercising and taking dietary precautions we can reduce the severity or even the occurrence of diabetes. We can also improve the quality of our lives by making positive choices regarding health factors that are within our control, such as minimizing the use of alcohol and tobacco products.
- **Relationships:** We have little control over whether our friends and loved ones will suffer debilitating diseases or die, but we can do much to nurture them while they are still with us. Further, we can find ways to connect meaningfully with others we meet later in life, and we can also learn to enjoy the relationship with ourselves, being alone and traveling our own inner byways.

Do you believe that you can have a positive influence on the quality of your life? Do you take time to recognize and celebrate your accomplish-ments and reward yourself for your efforts and the progress you are making? Do you try to enhance your well-being? Do you practice saying no when you are asked to engage in activities that are not appropriate for you? Do you get as much pleasure from reflection, or "being," as you do from action, or "doing"? Do you help other aging people improve the quality of their lives?

To answer these questions positively, we need to confront our fears, put them in realistic perspective, and believe that we have the potential to improve the quality of our lives and the lives of others. Most of us are fully able to respond to the challenges that stand in the way of a quality life, but to make our older years more meaningful,

> *One always has time enough, if one will apply it well.*
> —Wolfgang von Goethe

> *I believe that anyone can conquer fear by doing the things he fears to do, provided he keeps doing them until he gets a record of success.*
> —Eleanor Roosevelt

> *Life is like a ten-speed bike. Most of us have gears we never use.*
> —Charles Schultz

we need to believe in our ability to do so. Our attitudes impact how we experience life and how we age. How else can we account for the fact that the same conditions diminish one person while another person grows? It's how we see things that matter or, to put it differently, it's what's in us, not what's out there, that counts.

> *The thing you are ripening toward is the fruit of your life.*
> —Stewart Edward White

Planning for Resiliency

Resiliency doesn't just happen. It is achieved inch by inch, with effort and the abiding belief that we can lead meaningful lives. We can live resiliently if we learn from experiences, clarify our hopes, develop a vision, and create a basic plan for our future. It's not about creating a blueprint or a detailed set of rules. It's about developing of a general set of overall beliefs, expectations, and guidelines for our behaviors.

> *Life is what happens to you while you are making other plans.*
> —John Lennon

Life shifts and changes in its own mysterious ways. We need to be able to move with life's rhythms in order to age well. Our older years are a journey, and that's when we need to come to grips with questions like these: Who am I? Who am I becoming? Who will come along with me? Following some basic guidelines can help us take the journey.

> *Dare. Go toward life. Take chances. Reach out to what you most fear. Develop the habit of daring life so that you will not look back with regret at what you have not done.*
> — Donald M. Murray

Get Over Your Resistance to Change

Change means letting go of beliefs and behaviors that we are comfortable with but may no longer be appropriate or effective for us at this stage of life. Change means leaving the shore and heading out to sea before we fully realize or perhaps even vaguely know where we

> *To die unchanged, except in body, is to have lived in vain.*
> —Hugh L'Anson Faussett

are going. Most of us will probably experience uncertainty and a sense of disequilibrium as we move out of our comfort zones, take risks, gather information, and learn new skills.

> *A setback only paves the way for a comeback.*
> —Evander Holyfield

We need to be careful not to judge ourselves harshly or conclude that we have failed if we fall short of our goals when we try to change. After all, if everything goes smoothly, it probably means that we haven't been stretching ourselves. Coping with change may be difficult, but there are things that we can do to make the journey less painful:

- ***Be realistic about expectations.*** Start with small steps and work up to a full agenda over time. If we want to strengthen our muscles, we should start with five- or ten-pound weights, not fifty- or one-hundred-pound weights. The same is true about building our confidence: be realistic; don't overreach.

  > *I was taught that the way of progress is neither swift nor easy*
  > —Marie Curie

- ***Start with things that are positive and attractive.*** Building a solid, positive platform is more motivating than having to break bad habits. For example, we will probably be more enthused about learning a hobby than we will be about quitting smoking. With time, accomplishments, and growing self-confidence, it will become easier to confront our more difficult challenges.

- ***Keep it simple.*** For example, for most of us it would probably be a lot easier to explore spirituality by participating in a guided workshop than it would be to try to read the many volumes that compare and contrast what the world's great religions teach about it.

  > *In all sound efforts to do something new, it is important to remember the principle of the small steps.*
  > —Fritz Kunkel and Roy E. Dickerson

- ***Enjoy the journey because it is as important as the outcomes.*** We learn as much from the efforts that we expend and the insights we gain through our experiences as we do from the goals we attain. Life is an amazing journey, an adventure that enriches those who take it.

> *You cannot discover new oceans unless you have the courage to lose sight of the shore.*
>
> —Tibetan proverb

Get Real about the Starting Place

We need to assess our strengths and our weaknesses as we journey into our older years. In particular, we have to:

- Realize that we have had many experiences that may be helpful, but they may not adequately prepare us for the life we will lead when we grow older.
- Recognize that the skills we developed to meet challenges when we became adults, raised families, and conducted our work roles may need to be modified and refined to fit our changing situation. Some skills may not transfer and others may need to be retooled.
- Focus on developing new abilities that may not have seemed relevant earlier in life, but are becoming important now. For example, we need to figure out how to create our own boundaries to replace externally imposed boundaries that may no longer be relevant, learn how to channel our energies and capabilities into newly defined meaningful activities, and explore our connections with spirituality.
- "Getting real" means accepting the fact that we are amateurs. We have much to learn about our aging years. We have to come to terms with being strangers in a strange new land. Enjoy the journey and don't be embarrassed that you don't know everything you need to know.

> *Perseverance is essential ... You don't persevere without a vision.*
>
> —Dr. Lester Thurow

Mike M. Milstein

Develop Your Vision

What is your vision of a high-quality older life? What are its major components? Does it focus on fulfillment and personal growth? Does it include connecting and relating with others? Does it emphasize service? Does it encompass reflection, solitude, and self-knowledge? Does it allow for extensive travel? Does it include informal and formal growth and development experiences? What about exercise? What about a good diet? What about health maintenance?

We also need to think about whether our vision is realistic. Is it feasible? Is it truly what we want? Is it challenging? Does it serve as a useful foundation for the development of goals and actions?

Of course, there is no one best vision of a high-quality life. A vision that is attractive and challenging to one person may not resonate at all for another person. Each of us needs to reflect about what we want our lives to be like and create a meaningful vision that fits our own needs and hopes.

Visioning is the starting place of the planning process. If we start with where we want to go, we can then figure out what we need to do to get there. The clearer we are about what we want, the more energized we will be about putting in the effort it takes to get there.

> *You don't get to choose how you're going to die. Or when. You can only decide how you're going to live. Now.*
> —Joan Baez

> *Creating a vision forces us to take a stand for a preferred future.*
> —P. Block

> *Tell me what you pay attention to and I will tell you who you are.*
> —Ortega y Gasset

> *Life can only be understood backwards, but it must be lived forwards.*
> —Soren Kierkegaard

> ## Exercise: Clarifying Your Vision
>
> What does your vision of a quality older life look like? Putting your thoughts on paper is a good way of becoming clearer about your hopes and expectations.
>
> 1. Identify five or more key elements of your quality older life.
>   A.
>   B.
>   C.
>   D.
>   E.
>
> 2. When you think you have captured the important elements, try writing a vision statement that encompasses them.
>
> 3. You may want to edit your statement a few times to make sure it is both clear and appropriate for you.

ACTUALIZE YOUR VISION

Once you have clarified a vision that feels right, it's time to figure out how to actualize it. A sequence of steps that can guide you from visioning to living your vision includes creating meaningful goals, identifying strategies to achieve them, and monitoring and assessing your progress.

> *Even if you are on the right track, you'll get run over if you just sit there.*
> —Will Rogers

Create Meaningful Goals

Goals are nothing more than descriptions of specific outcomes that you want to achieve to bring your vision to life. To serve this purpose they need to be:

- Stated clearly, preferably in writing, so you understand what you expect to do.
- Positive, so you will make the efforts to achieve them.
- Measurable, so you know whether you are making progress.

- Time-bound so you know whether you have reached them. To maintain momentum, it is useful to develop *short-term goals,* which are like stepping-stones, framed to be achieved within weeks or months; *mid-term goals,* which are like marking posts, intended to be realized in a year or two; and *long-term goals,* which require concentrated effort over the long haul and are only attained after a significant length of the journey.

For example, a long-term goal may be to be a lifelong learner. To stay focused on this overall intent, it would be helpful to create short-term goals, like reading relevant books or taking relevant workshops, and mid-term goals that may take a year or so to achieve, like finishing a course of studies or a college degree. Meeting your short-term goals helps build self-confidence and a sense of forward movement. Achieving mid-term goals builds on these positive outcomes, providing positive evidence of meaningful progress.

> *The future is not someplace we are going, but one we are creating.*
> —John Schaar

Identify Strategies to Achieve Your Goals

Chapters 3 through 8 provided descriptions of many strategies that can be applied to promote resiliency. The goals that you create in pursuit of your vision come to life when you sort through and select strategies that can help you reach them. Remember, however, that each of us is unique. We are likely to have different goals, different life situations, and different personalities. Take care to select the strategies that are right for you. How should you go about deciding which strategies best serve your needs? The following questions may help you make good choices:

> *The "silly" question is the first intimation of some totally new development.*
> —Whitehead

- Does it fit your goals?
- Does it have the potential to help you meet you goal?
- Are you likely to commit to the time, energy, and resource costs that will be required?

Resilient Aging

- Do you have the ability to apply it? If not, can you learn how to do so?
- Are there other strategies that might work as well or better for you?

Strategies can be helpful for the achievement of multiple resiliency related goals. Therefore, as we plan, we need to think about ways of maximizing the value of the strategies we select and apply.

Monitor and Assess Your Progress

If you don't keep track of where you are going, you are likely to end up somewhere else! When you take a trip, especially if you are going someplace for the first time, you need a map to figure out the best route as well as the highway markers and road signs that will help you stay on our intended route. In similar fashion, when you decide about life goals you want to achieve, you need strategies to pursue them, as well as measures that help you know whether you are on target and how far you have come. You may also need to fine-tune or even change your strategies if you fall short of your expectations.

> *We have to water, cultivate, and weed on a regular basis if we're going to enjoy the harvest. The difference between our own active involvement as gardeners and neglect is the difference between a beautiful garden and a weed patch.*
> —Stephen R. Covey

How will you know you are achieving your goals? What are your criteria? Probably the most important thing to do is trust your own judgment. Do you feel better, more enthused, more satisfied? Can you identify behaviors that indicate that you are moving toward your goals? Assessment of progress might vary along the following continuum:

- ***Things are going the wrong way.*** It feels as if you are going backward.
- ***There is no change.*** It feels as if things are no different than they were.

> *If at first you don't succeed, you're running about average.*
> —M. H. Alderson

- ***I'm more aware and experimenting.*** It feels as if you are focused and on the move.
- ***There is evidence of change.*** You feel different, and you are beginning to do things differently.
- ***There is significant progress***: Many things are in place, and it looks as if you are going to make it!

As a check on your judgment, it may be a good idea to get feedback from others you trust. Do they see any differences in your attitudes or your behaviors? Do they believe that you are growing and developing? If so, in what ways?

The information that you gather from introspection and feedback from others can help you decide about next steps. If you are on course, you may want to continue to do what you are doing. If it looks like things aren't working well, you may need to consider modifying your strategies or perhaps applying different ones. If you are way off course, you may even need to reflect about whether your vision or your goals are realistic.

> *Our greatest glory consists not in merely falling, but in rising every time we fall.*
> —Ralph Waldo Emerson

KEEP THE VISION ALIVE

There are many ways that you can enhance the potential to live the visions you create. These include enlisting support, celebrating achievements, and repeating the cycle of activities so you keep developing while you continue to learn.

Enlist Support

Ultimately, you are responsible for managing your own life, but you can enhance your growth and development if you enlist the support of others. You can turn to family members, friends, community members, and caregivers for information, ideas, and encouragement. Connecting with others who believe in you and encourage you to achieve your goals can make a big difference. Knowing that others care reminds you that you are worthy and part of something bigger than yourself.

How do you mobilize this support? First and foremost, you need to

Resilient Aging

be supportive of others if you expect to be supported by them. Support is a mutual dynamic. When people believe you care, and that you will be there for them when they are in need, it is much more likely that they will be there to support you. As the golden rule reminds us, do unto others as you would have them do unto you. Second, you need to make your needs known. This requires that you let others know that you want to grow and develop. It also means being clear about your goals and being able to communicate them effectively. If you let others know about your needs and where you are heading, they are more likely to accompany you on the journey.

> *Trust yourself in the deep, uncharted waters. When there is a storm it is safer in the open sea. If you stay too near the dock you will get beaten to death.*
>
> —Sam Keen

Celebrate

As you make progress toward your goals, it is important to mark your achievements. Celebrating them reminds you and others that you have done what you set out to do and confirms your growth. Some ways to promote celebrating include:

- **Rituals and Rites of passage** that mark a change of status. A rite of passage might be a formal event that is conducted by a group, such as a graduation ceremony to mark the completion of a course of studies. It can also be individually created and conducted, such as when couples create their own marriage vows.
- **Awards Ceremonies** sponsored by groups and organizations to recognize achievements of members or other individuals. These are special events at which some tangible form of recognition is awarded to deserving individuals. For example, community volunteers' efforts are often recognized with a certificate or a plaque.
- **Self-Rewards.** These are special gifts you give yourself when you make significant progress toward important goals. They can be ways of celebrating goal achievement, motivating yourself to continue to pursue goals, or encouraging you to move on to other goals. Self-rewards vary widely and should be based on

relevance. For example, depending on your interests, they might focus on travel, time to relax and kick back, tickets to a concert or the theater, new clothes, or a dinner out.

Repeat the Cycle

Hopefully you are on your way to a more resilient life. You have a vision of what you want your life to be like. You have developed relevant goals and implemented strategies that can move you toward your goals. You are gaining confidence, learning from your experiences, and consolidating your gains.

It's important to build on these gains and keep the momentum up so you can live your vision. For example, one aspect of your vision might be to

> *The best way to predict the future is to create it.*
> —Peter Druker

connect meaningfully with others who are at your life stage, and a goal you may have chosen to do so is to participate in a variety of community-based volunteer groups. You may be making wonderful progress and are feeling good about what you have accomplished. If so, you may want to think about expanding your scope of participation to include other connecting possibilities. Or you may be satisfied with what you have accomplished and want to turn your thoughts and energies on to other goals that are also important to you.

The point is that we need to continue focusing on growth and development. By repeating the cycle of goal setting, strategy development, monitoring, and achievement, we enhance the probability of moving toward increased resiliency. If we don't, we may become fixed in place or even slide backward.

Keep Learning and Changing

The challenges we have to deal with as we age require us to keep growing, developing, and changing if we hope to manage life's transitions and remain resilient. For those of us who are fortunate to live long enough, there are three key transitions that will impact our vision, goals, and actions.

> *There is nothing more remarkable in the life of Socrates than that he found time in his old age to learn to dance and play on instruments and thought it time well spent.*
> —Michel de Montaigue

- ***The transition into retirement:*** Coming to terms with the end of our working years, if we stop working for pay, and preparing for life after retirement.
- ***The transition from retirement into our young-old years:*** Experimenting with the pace, rhythm, and focus of life after retirement, while we are still healthy, physically mobile, and able to engage in many physical activities.
- ***The transition from our young-old years into our old-old years:*** Learning to live with fewer options as our health and physical stamina decrease and discovering how to be more reflective and tap into the spiritual and wisdom worlds that are more available to us when we have to slow down and become more sedentary.

> *There is nothing more beautiful than an unadorned old face with the lines that tell a story, a story of life that has been lived with some fullness.*
> —Helen Hayes

IN CLOSING

We started our journey with a review of the historical shifts in the aging experience and a description of the myths that, for so long, promoted negative thinking about aging and created barriers to aging with resilience. We went on to explore the positive shifts in thinking about aging and the many breakthroughs over the past few decades that have led many of us to be more enthusiastic about the possibilities of aging with resilience. Not only has longevity expanded rapidly, but there is the increasing probability that many of us will be able to remain healthy and grow and develop during these additional years.

> *Two roads diverged in a wood, and I—I took the one less traveled by and that has made all the difference.*
> —Robert Frost

In fact, we are living in a time when the rules of aging are being rewritten. The information about aging that has recently become available to us is extensive and expanding at a rapid rate. Undoubtedly, there will be further breakthroughs in areas such as health, medicine, psychology, spirituality, the development and uses of our resources, and the possibilities of alternative housing arrangements. Our potential to live our older lives with resilience will undoubtedly be enhanced as these positive changes take place.

We are living in an extraordinary time. Negative beliefs about aging are in retreat, and positive beliefs are in the ascendancy. Our challenge is to take advantage of the growing possibilities of aging with resilience. As we come to the end of the book, it is my hope that you will accept the challenge to live your older years with resilience—and to continue to do so until your earthly existence comes to an end.

> *Youth is a gift of nature; aging is a work of art.*
> —Anonymous

> *Hope is itself a species of happiness, and perhaps the chief happiness which the world affords.*
> —Dr. Johnson

References

Albom, Mitch. *Tuesdays with Morrie.* New York: Doubleday, 1997.

Anderson, Barbara Gallatin. *The Aging Game.* New York: McGraw-Hill Book Company, 1979.

Blum, Deborah. "Finding Strength." *Psychology Today*, May–June 1998.

Carter, Jimmy. *The Virtues of Aging.* New York: The Library of Contemporary Thought, 1998.

Chopra, Deepak. *Grow Younger, Live Longer.* New York: Harmony Books, 2001.

Cockerham, William C.. *The Aging Society.* Englewood Cliffs, New Jersey: Prentice Hall, 1991.

Coles, Robert. *Old and on Their Own.* New York: DoubleTake, 1997.

Cohen, Gene D.. *The Creative Age.* New York: Quill, 2001.

Cox, Harold G.. *Later Life,* 3rd edition. Englewood Cliffs, NJ: Prentice Hall, 1993.

Dass, Ram. *Still Here.* New York: Riverhead Books, 2000.

Dychtwald, Ken and Flower, Joe. *Age Wave.* Los Angeles: Jeremy P. Tarcher, Inc., 1989.

Erikson, Erik H. Erikson, Joan M., and Kivnick, Helen Q..*Vital Involvem ent in Old Age.* New York: W.W. Norton and Company 1994.

Frankl, Viktor E. *Man's Search for Meaning.* New York: Washington Square Press, 1959.

Friedan, Betty. *The Fountain of Age.* New York: Simon and Schuster, 1993.

Higgins,.Gina O'Connell *Resilient Adults.* San Francisco: Jossey-Bass Publishers, 1994.

Hillman, James. *The Force of Character.* New York: Random House, 1999.

Hudson, Frederic M.. *The Adult Years.* San Francisco: Jossey-Bass Publishers, 1991.

Kidder, Tracy. *Old Friends.* New York: Houghton Mifflin Company, 1993.

Kingsolver, Barbara. *High Tide in Tucson.* New York: Harper Perennial, 1995.

Levine, Stephen. *A Year to Live.* New York: Bell Tower, 1997.

Levy, Becca, Slade, Martin D. Kunkel, Suzanne R., and Kasl, Stanislav V. "Longevity Increased by Positive Self Perceptions of Aging." *Personality and Social Psychology,* August 2002, Vol. 83, No. 2.

Levinson, Daniel J. *The Seasons of a Man's Life.* New York: Ballantine Books, 1978.

Milstein, Mike M. and Henry, Doris Annie *Leadership for Resilient Schools and Communities,* 2nd edition. Thousand Oaks, California: Corwin Press, 2008.

Moody, Harry R. *The Five Stages of the Soul.* New York: Anchor Books, 1997.

Nuland, Sherwin B. *How We Die: Reflections on Life's Final Chapter.* New York: Vintage Books, 1955.

Perls, Thomas T. and Silver, Margery Hutter. *Living to 100.* New York: Basic Books, 1999.

Pipher, Mary. *Another Country.* New York: Riverhead Books, 1999.

Rowe, John W. and Kahn, Robert L.. *Successful Aging.* New York: Dell Publishing, 1999.

Schachter-Shalomi, Zalman and Mille,r Ronald S.. *From Age-ing to Sage-ing.* New York: Warner Books, 1995.

Seligman, Martin E. P.. *Authentic Happiness.* New York: Free Press, 2002.

Seligman, Martin E. P. *Learned Optimism*, New York, Pocket Books, 1990

Sheehy, Gail. *New Passages.* New York: Random House, 1995.

Sheehy, Gail. *Passages.* New York: P. Dutton, 1974.

Vaillant, George E.. *Aging Well.* Boston: Little, Brown and Company, 2002.

Werner, Emmy E. and Smith, Ruth S.. *Overcoming the Odds.* Ithaca, NY: Cornell University Press, 1992.

Lightning Source UK Ltd.
Milton Keynes UK
19 October 2010

161577UK00001B/53/P

9 781440 175886